Pinpointing and Shedding Generational Curses

By Carol J. Long

Secrets of the Cocoon
For People in Metamorphosis

Xulon PRESS

chrysalis, bear, and butterfly drawings by Erin Harman at erin_harman@aol.com

www.xulonpress.com

Dedicated to the memory of Harry Bascom,
counselor at Wycliffe Bible Translators,
who directed me to a neutral environment
where I could pull back temporarily
from the mainstream of life
to construct a new mindset

Acknowledgements

I'm grateful for my parents who made every conceivable sacrifice to give their five offspring the very best possible start in life.

My thanks go to my patient and enduring husband who has been my sounding board.

I thank my pastors whose mature teaching and mentoring have helped bring me to the place where I can minister to others.

I thank B. Kay Coulter (who is both an author and an editor) for edits, formatting, and suggestions related to content.

My thanks go out to God that He has not left us in this world without a purpose.

Contents

Dear Friend,

Have you been struggling with failure? Are you caught in an addiction? Have you felt as if you're having a nervous breakdown? Did you suffer abuse but got no closure? Have you noticed a negative pattern, such as anger, in your family? Do you dream but not move forward? If you answered *yes* to any of these, I believe this book is for you.

Doesn't it amaze you that people of wealth, who can get the most expensive rehab in the country, often don't get lasting help? We read about them in the headlines once it's too late. We watch their expensive funerals on television. We hear about movie stars cycling in and out of rehab.

Lasting freedom—deliverance, actually—requires something money can't buy. First, one must identify the culprits, the roots. Then comes the spiritual warfare involved in removing roots. Our weapon resources include the Holy Spirit Himself, the power in the blood of Jesus, the power in the name of Jesus, and the living Word of God at work. Let's also not underestimate the power of confession and of praying for each other. One big tool is your own mouth; with it you can release God's power into your life (or the enemy's destruction). You can take charge in the realm of faith.

You will find that the secular community is often reluctant to talk about psychological or physical medical problems in spiritual terms. Actually, the spiritual realm has not changed since the days of Jesus's earthly ministry. It is true that we have had breakthroughs in areas of medicine, including psychology; but let's be very honest for a minute about depression, psychosis, and conditions such as diabetes or cancer. We often need a miracle, not only a treatment. Many treatments have negative side effects and may not be fully successful.

I talk regularly with female inmates, many of whom say they feel overwhelmed, as if on the verge of a nervous breakdown. Others say they *hope* they will stay clean from drugs when they get out of jail, but they lack confidence. Many want to get out immediately to see their children, but are they ready to effectively parent these children? Many of these women are on prescription drugs for nervous disorders, and many suffer from serious diseases. The problems that sideline people in life didn't develop in one day, and they won't be solved in one day. However, a fresh mindset can begin today. This mindset is that God's power is available to heal and deliver.

A basic key to spiritual freedom is being aware of generational curses in the bloodline. You can also identify negative behaviors, conditions, and mindsets that often accompany these curses in a family. Let's get one thing straight: we are not here to bash or belittle family members. However, it is wise to pinpoint the work of the enemy. It is crucial to identify negative patterns that have come down the family line if they have affected us or our children. Once the patterns are identified, they can be renounced. We have authority over all the ability of the enemy.

In this interactive book, in addition to doing some of your own closet cleaning, you'll watch four other lives unfold, the lives of four people who floundered in spiritual valleys—namely, a nervous breakdown, addiction to meth, childhood victimization, and addiction to alcohol. These four adults will name generational curses that plagued their family lines, accompanying behaviors and conditions, and the negative mindsets. They will share some relevant medical or personality details. Most importantly, they will list the vital choices they made in their turnaround. These four testimonies are completely authentic.

If you have accepted Jesus as Savior, then you will be exercising your rights. If you have not yet accepted Jesus as Savior, you can do that now. Turn to the section at the end of the book, labeled "Helps", and follow His open invitation.

True success in life is to know Jesus and to become like Him. May you find in these pages the real you, the peaceful you that wants to emerge, the *you* that may have been deterred by wrong thinking. It's all in how one views himself. Do you realize that God made you just the way He wanted you to be—that there is *nothing wrong with you*? I got mad the first time my pastor preached that there is nothing wrong with us. It took me many months to realize it was true. You are you. You are unique and special for a reason, for a destiny. Anyone can shed the layers of wrong influence and thinking and settle into the satisfying place of being loved and favored by God

You can start today to benefit from root-level, Holy Spirit rehab. You are destined to win. It's a spiritual battle, and you have all the tools you need. You can identify the tentacles at the core of your failures, cover them in the blood of Jesus, and pull them out by the root. The Holy Spirit, your Helper, will be right beside you, and in you.

You can face any pattern in your life, for, "There is no fear in love. But perfect love drives out *fear,* because fear has to do with punishment. The one who fears is not made perfect in love" (1 John 4:18).

Chapter 1

Secrets of the Cocoon

Do you ever wish you could just wrap yourself in a cocoon? Maybe you would like to step back temporarily from the world. Do you wonder if you will ever be able to fly, a radiant display of God's handiwork? Be encouraged. This book is for people in metamorphosis. For a moment, let's get inside a real cocoon and see what happens when a "slug" gets ready for flight.

Consider the humble pupa. At birth, a caterpillar eats its way out of the egg, then eats the leaf it was laid on, then eats its way around until it is in the last pupa stage, perhaps only six feet or so from its hatching spot. These eating machines eat up to twenty-seven thousand times their own weight in leaves. They live out five stages, shedding skin each time they expand.

A butterfly in the caterpillar stage actually becomes its own cocoon, or chrysalis. Once a pupa gets ready to transform, it sheds its skin for the last time; and its existing skin hardens into a shell. Enzymes are released, and the plump pupa begins to turn into total jelly inside this shell. Can you imagine your heart and liver and brain turning to jelly while you are still alive? Fortunately for the pupa, it houses little cell clusters that have been there since the very first pupa stage. These little cell clusters, or discs, which have been dormant, now feed on the gel and grow into body parts—a heart, a brain, a nervous system, muscles, and even wings. This potential for wings and a new heart was there from birth. Even though the pupa becomes fully developed, it may not chew its way out of the chrysalis for months if the weather is dry or the winter is harsh.

Once the new creature emerges and dries its wings, its existence consists of flight and nectar. Whereas the plump pupa had navigated only a few feet from its birthplace, this winged beauty can now fly up to one thousand miles (in some cases, two thousand miles), laying eggs and pollinating fruits, vegetables, and flowers over continents. Its influence magnifies exponentially.

The Bible says that a Christian also is a new creation (2 Corinthians 5:17). Sometimes we have to claim that by faith. We may exhibit behaviors that don't seem renewed. We may feel as if we are inching along in life like a slug, going nowhere, weighted down. This is the right time to cocoon with God, surrounding ourselves with a kind of "royal gel", which is the Word of God. Getting into a cocoon with God is a choice. It's like saying, "God, I'm here to line myself up with your blueprint." Just as the pupa loses half its body weight during metamorphosis, a Christian may have to shed some baggage too, making room for the newness in God. For humans, the bonus feature is that we can cocoon with God more than once.

Just like the pupa, we have little packets of potential that can be realized, but only with the power that is stored in the Word. When we soak in the Word, our clusters of potential are energized by truth. People who knew us before may no longer recognize us, but our potential for wings had been there all along.

Let's talk about success and influence. The caterpillar may travel only six feet from its hatching spot as it stuffs itself into obesity. This can remind us of a person who is dealing with addictions or life's traumas. He or she may seem very self-absorbed, having narrow horizons, just trying to survive. Once a person is transformed by the Word of God, he or she may now escape the small world, get airborne, and share the love and healing power of Christ all along life's highways, or should I say "airways". Defying gravity can be exhilarating.

Turning into mush

I can tell you from personal experience that turning to mush can be frightening for a human. As I entered my thirties, my mindset was so distorted that I could no longer move forward. I reached a place where I could not function, suffering what people then might have called a "nervous breakdown". I had to let go of my old thinking or crumble, literally. I was surprised that the sun actually kept rising and that the world was still turning as I started to let go of pride and self-effort. The whole experience was deeply humbling. I am sharing it now in hopes that someone who is battling despair will latch on to hope, even it if feels like hanging upside down from a twig for awhile.

For the human, thought patterns determine destiny. Our thought patterns determine our mental health, our happiness, our ability to get along with others, and our success. The Bible says that we are made in God's image. I take that to mean that we are spirit beings, as God is, and that we are intelligent and creative, as He is. If our thinking is badly distorted about our own selves, we are headed for trouble.

If you trace wrong thinking to its source, you will probably backtrack into the environment in which one's thinking formed. (What if that caterpillar had found some bad leaves?) If a person's environment included harmful behaviors, conditions, or words, this could be evidence of generational curses at work. The theme of blessings and curses permeates the Bible. Even in modern times, an understanding of blessings and curses is essential. Some families are characterized by patterns of blessings, and some by patterns of curses. Most families display some of both.

If you suspect that oppression, failure, weakness, or disease has plagued your family line, here is a handbook to help you shake that off. There is no fear in this process because God has already made provision for complete success in Jesus. So, if you are ready to cocoon with the Holy Spirit and get some new wings, let's look at the reality of how curses can affect a family line. Be prepared to let some thought patterns turn to mush. God didn't intend for people to remain in the pupa stage.

Just as the pupa does not exit from the chrysalis until conditions are right, we may have to draw aside at times in life to examine, in an unhurried way, what is really going on. (When I spent several months in a mental ward, I was examining my life, my motives, and my goals.) If I soak myself in the Word of God, my little potential packets will form a new mind and heart in me; and I'll know when I am ready to get out and lift off. You may be in a jail cell, in a hospital, in a rehab unit, or simply in the confines of some bondage or mindset you would like shake off. Let the old pupa turn to mush so you can get on with your potential. Pinpointing and shedding generational curses can pave the way for right thinking—flight mentality.

Maybe you are not actually struggling with failures, but you do seem to be bound by limitations. Are there objectives you have wanted to attempt, but you never seem to start them? Do you wonder why you dream but never go toward your dream? You may have a mindset of limitation that needs to turn to mush so you can get on with the most exciting chapter of your life.

Chapter 2

Bible Background on Blessings and Curses

These Curses Shall Follow Them

As you attempt to get a handle on why you are not where you want to be in life, an understanding of generational curses can be liberating. We don't blame our ancestors for our problems, but we can learn about our sins and failures by looking at theirs. God has great plans for families; he has passed down gifts to you which can be developed to help others. However, there is a price to be paid for the sins of the fathers. Jesus actually *paid* that price with His blood; but the blood must be *applied* to demonic influences. If we don't get in step with Jesus's atoning sacrifice, we might keep paying the price for the demonic curses that operated through our ancestors. Jesus took every curse upon himself. Why pass up this provision?

Let's get one crucial point straight. God does not curse people. God loves us and wants to bless us. Curses are invited when God's laws are violated. When the Lord gave us His commandments, His intention was that we would honor Him by honoring the commandments. God does not punish people by putting curses on them. Jesus took the curse so that we would escape God's wrath. God is just and can't just ignore sin. That is why, in His love, He sent Jesus to atone for our sins.The Bible talks about the curses for disobedience, and blessings for obedience. This prophetic revelation about Jesus, given to Isaiah the prophet, describes the benefits that Jesus's sacrifice would bring to people suffering under the curses of sin, turmoil, or illness.

"But he was pierced for our transgressions,
he was crushed for our iniquities;
the punishment that brought us peace was upon him,
and by his wounds we are healed."
Isaiah 53:5

Where do curses come from? Let's go back to Exodus 20 where God first revealed to Moses the Ten Commandments, or rules for living. Here is a paraphrase. Notice that four of the commandments relate to worshiping God: (1) there is one God; (2) have no idols; (3) do not take God's name in vain; and (4) honor the Sabbath. The other six commandments define our relationships with people. Jesus said that loving God and loving others would sum up all the "Law and the Prophets" (Matthew 22:40).

God knew the Law could never be followed to the letter! All through Scripture, God says that the Law simply makes us aware of our sin. All the blood sacrifices in the Old Testament were really pointing ahead to one perfect sacrifice. God was paving the way in history for a time when man would throw himself on the mercy of God through Jesus. Only by grace through faith can we measure up. It's the free gift of "righteousness," and Jesus paid for it with His blood, as we see in Hebrews 9:22. "In fact, the law requires that nearly everything be cleansed with blood, and without the shedding of blood there is no forgiveness."

Looking at Exodus chapter 20 and Deuteronomy chapter 28, we read that worshiping idols or practicing disobedience can invite curses into a family line.

> You shall not make for yourself an image in the form of anything in heaven above or on the earth beneath or in the waters below. You shall not bow down to them or worship them; for I, the LORD your God, am a jealous God, punishing the children for the sin of the parents to the third and fourth generation of those who hate me, but showing love to a thousand generations of those who love me and keep my commandments. Exodus 20:4-6

Making an image and bowing down to it constitutes idol worship. How we spend our time and money shows whether we have idols or not. The above verse makes it very clear that practicing idol worship or breaking other commandments can bring punishment to three or four following generations. You may say, "Yes, but that was in the Old Testament." It was; and the only way we come out from under curses even today is through the blood of Jesus, and through knowing how to call on the power in the blood. This is part of the new covenant.

Look again at the positive side of that passage in Exodus 20. God shows mercy to *thousands* of offspring if we love Him and keep His commandments. We can really change things around in our own family line! I made a decision some years ago that I wasn't going to let the enemy rob my giftings and health the way I've seen him rob the giftings and health of some people in my ancestry. I'm claiming the fact that Jesus paid for my destiny with His.

Blessings and Curses That Can Visit a Family Line

In Deuteronomy 28:1-14 we find a list of specific blessings that result from obeying God. In verses 15 through 68, we find curses which come from disobeying; and God specifically says that children to the third and fourth generations will be punished for the sins of their fathers. This makes sense. It's a way of holding people accountable for their sins. Perhaps your ancestors did their very best, but what if the whole clan has been laboring under some very negative patterns? Even Christians fall, and that is why we need forgiveness. In Romans, Paul wrote that "all have sinned and fall short of the glory of God" (Romans 3:23). There is no perfect family.

We might be reaping the toxic fruits of our ancestors' past sins. The Bible states that a curse doesn't come without a cause. "As the bird by wandering, as the swallow by flying, so the curse causeless shall not come" (Proverbs 26:2 KJV). We may not know the whole story about those who came before us. Someone may have missed the mark and started a curse. Grandpa Joe may have meant well, but he may have opened a can of worms. Fortunately, the apostle John wrote that "if we confess our sins, he is faithful and just to forgive us our sins, and to cleanse us from all unrighteousness" (1 John 1:9 KJV). We can claim freedom from any sin pattern, no matter where it started. Again, there may be a pattern of oppression or sin in my family line, but that doesn't mean I have to buy into it. I can't say that the devil made me do it.

But I'm very religious. How could I be under a curse?

Let's discuss very religious people for a moment. Do you ever wonder why some people go to church their whole lives but never lead anyone to Christ, never see anyone healed when they pray, and never see anyone delivered under their ministry? Is it possible these people are serving God out of their intellect and not really walking in the power of the Spirit? I think we can all benefit from taking a close look at the realm of curses and blessings that Jesus understood. Maybe you don't feel you are under a curse, but perhaps you're wondering why you don't experience the authority of Jesus. You might be surprised to discover what is holding you back. Don't be among those who think evil spirits bothered people only in Jesus's days of earthly ministry.

As for religion, it is a good thing to be spiritually-minded, but probably not to be religious. A sobering truth is that the most ritualistically religious people of Jesus's day sent Him to the cross. It was His destiny to go to the cross, but religious people ordered the deed.

Blessings vs. curses

Here is a list of blessings found in Deuteronomy 28:1-14. These are the blessings that come from obeying the Lord and following his commandments:

children blessed, crops blessed, livestock blessed,
basket and kneading trough blessed, blessed coming and
going,
success over enemies, barns blessed, everything you put
your hand to blessed,
abundant prosperity, rain, work blessed, no borrowing,
being the head and not the tail
(paraphrased)

We could summarize by saying HEALTH, WEALTH, AND PROSPERITY!!

I have to tell you that these blessings can be ours today through Jesus Christ.

Now, here is a list of curses found in Deuteronomy 28:15-68 which result from disobedience. Notice that the list includes many curses affecting health, wellness, confidence, and success. I have condensed the phrases, but the terminology is straight from the Bible.

curses, confusion and rebuke in everything you put your hand to, diseases, wasting disease, fever and inflammation, scorching heat and drought, blight and mildew, sky over your head as bronze, ground beneath you as iron, rain of your country turned to dust and powder, being defeated before your enemies, boils of Egypt and tumors, festering sores and the itch, madness, blindness and confusion of mind, unsuccessful in everything you do, oppressed and robbed, pledged to be married to a woman but another takes her, building a house but not living in it, livestock and produce going to others, sons and daughters given to another nation, lack, dire poverty, suppression by enemies, slavery, fearful, plagues, prolonged disasters, severe and lingering illnesses, sickness and disaster, worship of other Gods, anxious mind, eyes weary with longing, despairing heart, constant suspense, terror

Again, these are the curses that would result from disobedience if we were under the Law. However, we are now under grace. We have been freed from the curse of the Law. Let's put the curses into categories. They would boil down to something like this:

DISEASE, LACK, CONFUSION, MADNESS, LACK OF SUCCESS, OPPRESSION, SLAVERY, PROLONGED DISASTERS, WEARINESS AND LONGING, SUSPENSE, TERROR, WORSHIP OF OTHER "GODS"

Do any of these things ring a bell for you? Not one of these curses is God's will for us. If you have accepted the atoning blood of Jesus, you are an heir in the kingdom of God; and you can walk in his victory. In today's world, the same blessings or curses can be found as were described in the book of Deuteronomy. God said that curses would follow a people of disobedience. We can be a people of obedience, cleansed in the atoning blood of Christ. We can literally choose to walk in the blessings of God. If curses have been attending our family lines, we can step out from under those curses. Jesus has paid for our sin nature. "God made him who had no sin to be sin for us, so that in him we might become the righteousness of God" (2 Corinthians 5:21).

We claim our righteousness by faith. We walk in obedience to the best of our ability, drawing on Christ's forgiveness. We don't go around sinning so we can draw on God's mercy. That would be what Dietrich Bonhoeffer called "cheap grace." We choose right living, and we do it by grace *through faith*. Because we are righteous by faith, we are removed from the curse that would have come from disobedience to the Law. "Christ hath redeemed us from the curse of the law, being made a curse for us: for it is written, Cursed is every one that hangeth on a tree" (Galatians 3:13).

Bible Accounts of Generational Patterns—lying, murder and idolatry vs. blessings

Let's consider first a story from the book of Genesis that many of us know well. In this account, a pattern of lying and deceit is clearly visible in a family line. To some, lying may not seem like a big sin; but the ninth commandment forbids lying. Lying and deception do not invite the blessing of God. In this story, many blessings are poured out on a family line; however, much heartache and confusion also come as a result of a generational pattern of bending the truth.

God promised the patriarch Abraham that his offspring would be as numerous as the stars in the sky or as the sand on the seashore. In other words, we would not be able to count Abraham's offspring. What really pleased God about Abraham was that he had been willing to sacrifice his only son Isaac on an altar, even though Abraham thought his later offspring were to come through Isaac. At the last moment, God provided a ram so that Isaac didn't have to die. Abraham had passed the test of faith and trust by taking his son onto the mountain to sacrifice him. It was blind obedience that sprang from faith. God loves faith. Paul wrote that Abraham's faith was "credited to him as righteousness" (Romans 4:3). Abraham showed proof of his faith; and in the next moment, God provided a ram to be sacrificed instead of a boy.

This boy Isaac grew up and married Rebekah. This couple had twins, Jacob and Esau. Jacob's male offspring would become the patriarchs after which the tribes of Israel would be named. God made good His promise to Abraham. However, along the way, there would be this spirit of deception which would keep raising its head; and Jacob especially would suffer much as a result, as we will see.

The first mention of this pattern of lying was with Abram in Genesis chapter 12. In a time of famine, Abram took Sarai into Egypt. Fearing that his life might be in danger because his wife was beautiful, he told Sarai to say she was his sister. It is true that she was his half sister, but she was also his wife. Sure enough, she wound up in Pharaoh's palace. However, such diseases came upon Pharaoh's household that he ordered that Sarai be returned to Abram. At a later time (after name changes), Abraham moved into a pagan region named Gerar and was again afraid that the men there would kill him in order to take his beautiful wife. To protect himself, he again lied and said that his wife was his sister. King Abimelech sent for Sarah, but the king's household fell under a curse of barrenness. To protect Sarah from defilement, God warned Abimelech in a dream not to touch her. The king returned Sarah to Abraham undefiled. In this way, God protected His covenant, since Sarah was later to bear Isaac, the son of promise.

When Isaac was grown, he took Rebekah to be his wife. Rebekah's grandfather Nahor was the brother of Isaac's father, Abraham. Nahor had a son named Bethuel who fathered Rebekah. Isaac and his wife Rebekah were related, though Rebekah was one generation younger than Isaac. During a famine, Isaac took Rebekah to the region of Gerar, which was still under the rule of a king named Abimelech. Fearing that the men of that region would kill him to get his wife, Isaac lied as his father had, saying that his wife was his sister. After King Abimelech saw Isaac caressing his wife, he returned her to her husband. He then made a decree that any man who touched Isaac's wife would be put to death.

Those accounts of fibbing may seem pretty tame, but the lying spirit gained momentum with Rebekah, this time springing out of favoritism. Isaac and Rebekah had twin sons, Jacob and Esau. Even in the womb, the babies jostled each other so much that Rebekah inquired of the Lord as to what it meant. God revealed to her that two nations were in her womb, and that the older would serve the younger. Esau was born first, then Jacob. Jacob came out grasping Esau's heal. They named him "Jacob" because that name meant "one who grasps." This was a play on words, which also figuratively meant "one who deceives." This label would prove itself to be true.

Jacob was the indoor type, able to cook. He was the favored son of his mother. Esau was the outdoor type, a hunter, and was favored by his father. Even though God had revealed to Rebekah that the older would serve the younger, it is interesting that this came about through deception.

Esau came in famished one day. Jacob had made some stew, and hungry Esau promised that Jacob could take his birthright if he would just give him some stew immediately. Esau ate the stew and went on his way. Esau had sold his birthright, in a moment of haste, for a meal.

Then it came time for the older son, Esau, to receive his blessing from his father Isaac, who was by this time old, blind, and about to die. Isaac called for his older son, Esau, telling him to go hunt and to prepare some wild game just before the blessing would be given to him. Rebekah secretly encouraged Jacob, her favored son, to act as if he had hunted for game. Quickly, Rebekah prepared a young goat, seasoning it to please Isaac. She and Jacob took it in to the aging Isaac. In order to disguise Jacob, Rebekah had covered his smooth arms with hairy skins. Jacob even wore Esau's clothes, which smelled of the field. Isaac questioned whether the voice was really that of Esau; but upon feeling the hairy arms and smelling the wild odor, he decided it must be Esau and gave his blessing. The blessing was much coveted because the Jews understood the power of words. The blessing had to do with health and prosperity.

Just after the blessing had been given to Jacob, Esau came in and realized his blessing had been stolen. Technically, he *had* sold his birthright for a single meal; but still, Jacob got the blessing by deceiving his father. When Isaac realized he had been fooled, he trembled violently. He then spoke words over Esau that no son wants to hear. He said, basically, that Esau would have a difficult life, living by the sword. Great hatred came into Esau's heart over this. Jacob, knowing that his brother intended to kill him, moved away to Paddan Aram, to live with his mother's brother, Laban. The seeds of deceit sown by Jacob and his mother would produce a harvest of more deceit.

Jacob took a fancy to Laban's younger daughter Rachel. He thought he married Rachel, but he woke up the next morning to find that he had slept with Leah, Rachel's older sister. Leah's father, Laban, explained that it was the custom to marry off the older daughter before the younger one. Why hadn't Laban openly told Jacob this in the first place? Maybe he feared he would never marry off Leah, who had what the Bible calls "weak eyes." Jacob went ahead and married Rachel also because he loved her. Thus, Laban had deceived Jacob; and Jacob now had two wives who were full sisters. In Leviticus 18:18 we read, "Do not take your wife's sister as a rival wife and have sexual relations with her while your wife is living." Though this law was given to Moses much later, we see that for Laban to trick Jacob into marrying Leah before he could marry Rachel was a move that would cause endless striving. All of her days, Leah labored to experience the affection which Jacob felt only for Rachel.

Jacob raised goats while living in Laban's household. In fact, he devised a method for breeding goats that caused his herds to multiply faster than those of Laban. He did not disclose his method to Laban. Eventually, Jacob took his wives, children, and herds and left Paddan Aram secretly. He was reconciled with his brother Esau and settled in Succoth.

Leah, who was not favored by Jacob, tried for years to gain his affection by bearing children for him. Rachel bore one son, Joseph; and Jacob favored Joseph above Leah's sons and made him a special coat. There were also other sons born to the servant maids of Jacob's wives. As time went on, all these other sons realized that they were not honored as much as Joseph, the one son of Rachel. To make matters worse, Joseph shared about his dreams in which it seemed that his brothers were bowing down to him.

The sons of Jacob practice deceit

Then came the greatest deception of all. One day, Jacob sent his young son Joseph out to check on his brothers in the field. When the brothers saw Jacob, they remembered his dreams and the special treatment he had received from their father. Their jealousy and resentment took full vent that day. They smeared goat's blood on Joseph's fancy colored coat and sold him as a slave. They lied to their father, implying that Joseph had been mauled by wild animals and that only his bloody coat had been found.

For years, Jacob mourned the alleged death of his favorite son. Later, Rachel had a second son; but she died in childbirth. Now Jacob had only his little son Benjamin to remind him of his wife Rachel whom he had loved. Even though all the older brothers eventually went to Egypt during a famine and discovered that their brother Joseph was alive, the Bible does not record that they ever confessed to their father that they had sold Joseph and smeared goat's blood on his coat. Joseph was sold at age seventeen and did not reconnect with his family until after age thirty. Jacob needlessly mourned the loss of his son for at least thirteen years.

Joseph tested his brothers in Egypt to see if they had changed. They did show remorse in that they strived to protect Rachel's second son, Benjamin, in Egypt. However, it is not recorded in Scripture that the brothers ever confessed to their father Jacob that they had lied about Joseph's disappearance and the bloody coat. We are left to assume that Jacob went to the grave not knowing that his older sons had lied to him, causing years of unnecessary grieving over a son that was thought to be dead. When Pharaoh of Egypt asked Jacob about his age, Jacob replied that his years had been "few and difficult" (Genesis 47:9). Possibly it was the pattern of deception in the family which had made Jacob's life particularly difficult. The one who was named "deceiver" suffered much due to lies.

Let's just review the suffering brought upon Jacob as a result of lying. He had to live with the knowledge that he had deceived his own father, Isaac, shortly before Isaac's death. Jacob was separated from his brother Esau for years as a result of this offense. His rival wives brought much strife into the household as a result of Laban's trickery. Later, Jacob's own sons lied to him about the disappearance of Joseph; and he grieved many years needlessly, thinking Joseph was dead. As far as we know, Jacob himself went to the grave never knowing the truth about the plot of his own sons in causing Joseph's disappearance.

There is a family in the Bible which displayed even more disturbing behaviors than the lying we just read about. In the records of the kings, we read of Queen Jezebel and her husband Ahab who left a trail of murder and idolatry, reaping destruction. Their daughter Athaliah also practiced treachery and met with disaster, as did her son.

For an example of a more positive generational mantle, we can look at Hannah in the book of First Samuel. Barren, she sought God with prayer and fasting. She did bear a son named Samuel who became a prophet of Israel. He was a godly son, "above reproach." Another story of blessing is the story of Ruth and Boaz, godly people who became the great-grandparents of King David. A New Testament example of generational blessing would be in the family line of Timothy, Paul's spiritual son, whose mother and grandmother are mentioned as having been people of "sincere faith" (2 Timothy 1:5).

Chapter 3

Your Profile
Background Check

Generational Curses

Generational curses are sometimes referred to as "generational spirits" or as "negative traits." Perhaps you don't believe in spirits. Jesus took authority over spirits all the time. He usually did this by speaking to them, commanding them to go. Many times he cast out more than one. Reading the four Gospels closely can help you realize that spirits exist. They have no power over a person unless one allows it because Jesus has triumphed over every force in heaven and on earth. Jesus wants us to rise up in His authority, in His name. He literally shares His authority with you and with me. "Behold, I give unto you power to tread on serpents and scorpions, and over all the power [ability] of the enemy: and nothing shall by any means hurt you" (Luke 10:19 KJV).

Some people like to get into a discussion as to whether or not a Christian can have a demon. I'm not going into that issue much here. If a Christian cannot have a demon, then it would seem that a Christian would never gossip, be in bondage to pornography, or murder, for example. I do believe that a Christian can open himself or herself to the demonic realm. However, in this book I am dealing primarily with spirits which come to oppress. Oppression comes when we listen to the lies of the enemy. It may come in the form of depression, bondage, or even illness. We don't have to put up with it. If we want to be free, we can be. Complete freedom involves warfare. Remember, there are many references in the Bible to the fact that we are in a war. Here is a great verse to explain why we must rise up every day and fight for our dominion. Notice that the word "against" occurs five times in this one verse. What are we fighting against? It's not people. Paul explains: "For our struggle is not against flesh and blood, but against the rulers, against the authorities, against the powers of this dark world and against the spiritual forces of evil in the heavenly realms" (Ephesians 6:12).

Jesus has given us power over all the *ability* of the enemy. In Ephesians 1, we read that Jesus has given us an inheritance which includes the authority He has, the authority over every force in heaven and earth. Paul wrote this amazing description of the authority we have over spiritual forces:

> "I pray that the eyes of your heart may be enlightened in order that you may know the hope to which he has called you, the riches of his glorious inheritance in his holy people, and his incomparably great power for us who believe. That power is the same as the mighty strength he exerted when he raised Christ from the dead and seated him at his right hand in the heavenly realms, far above all rule and authority, power and dominion, and every name that is invoked, not only in the present age but also in the one to come. And God placed all

things under his feet and appointed him to be head over everything for the church, which is his body, the fullness of him who fills everything in every way." Ephesians 1:18-23

Are you reading what I'm reading? We have the power of Jesus; and the power is for ruling over enemies, spiritual enemies.

The name "Satan" really just means "adversary." Your adversary, in some cases, will be a spirit that has tried to oppress one person after another in your family line. There are many levels of demonic spirits, some oppressing a person, some perhaps ruling over a city or even a nation. Here we are dealing with spirits that have simply come to roost in the family tree until they are driven off. Actually, in most cases, they are puny little spirits. It is their *lies* that can get a stronghold, especially when one's own mouth speaks out loud the old doubts and fears that have come into the mind through demonic suggestion. When people yield to the lies of evil spirits long enough, curses come upon them and upon their offspring. If a lying, demonic spirit is told to go, in the name of Jesus, it has to go. You can also declare that the lies that come to your mind simply aren't true. Maybe you have heard someone announce something like this: "Everyone in my family gets cancer by age forty." How about this: "Everyone in my family has the curse of bad knees." Here's one: "All the women in my family are fat." These are examples of people's tongues repeating the lies of the enemy. This invites a curse to stay.

If allowed to remain, curses can produce behaviors that are opposed to the fruit of the Spirit listed in Galatians chapter 5. The qualities we want to see in our lives are "love, joy, peace, forbearance, kindness, goodness, faithfulness, gentleness, and self-control" (Galatians 5:22-23).

Do these fruits describe your life? If not, what is in the way? Also, curses left unchecked can even lead to disease and death. There is absolutely nothing to fear, because evil spirits actually have no power. They have only the power over us which we allow them to exercise.

Identifying specific generational curses

Read through the list below to see if any of these pertain to you. Why not highlight or underline any that stand out? If there are a lot of issues you want to mark, perhaps put a star beside two or three you should deal with first. Remember through this whole process that you are not aiming to accuse people. You just want to identify the negative issues so you can walk in authority. Once you gain understanding, you can move ahead with confidence. You are not blaming people; you are identifying the work of the adversary. (Journal page #1 in the back is for your notes on this section.) If you feel overwhelmed because you find a lot of issues that have plagued your family line, take a more general approach and just believe God for an overhaul. Nothing is too hard for God. Check out this awesome truth which God revealed through Moses, found in Deuteronomy 28:13: "The LORD will make you the head, not the tail. If you pay attention to the commands of the LORD your God that I give you this day and carefully follow them, you will always be at the top, never at the bottom." That pretty much covers everything.

List #1

Generational Curses (generational spirits; strongholds)

This cannot possibly be a complete list of curses, but it does touch on the categories that we saw in Deuteronomy. Remember, our general categories were DISEASE, LACK, CONFUSION,

MADNESS, LACK OF SUCCESS, OPPRESSION, SLAVERY, PROLONGED DISASTERS, WEARINESS AND LONGING, SUSPENSE, TERROR, WORSHIP OF OTHER "GODS". Let's put some modern-day problem areas under these categories. These are sometimes referred to as "bloodline curses". Think of them as patterns that can run in a family.

A person must rise up to conquer such patterns. Some people might doggedly say that the Bible does not list all of the following as generational curses. I believe that when we see destructive patterns running in a family line, it is simply wise to acknowledge that there are curses at work. Why would I want to be a vehicle by which a negative pattern is perpetuated in my own family line? Below are some evidences of the main curses listed in Deuteronomy. Even though parents may invite curses into a family, adult children cannot continue to blame the parents for sins and other problems. At some point, we must choose to break free from patterns such as the following:

CONFUSION AND MADNESS
- anger
- rage
- fear, anxiety
- strife
- violence
- cruelty
- hatred
- rape
- murder

IDOLATRY, WORSHIP OF OTHER SO-CALLED "GODS"
- looking to statues, icons, relics, talismans, fetishes

- involvement in the occult—sorcery, witchcraft, astrology, spiritism, consulting "mediums", etc.
- cults (warning: cultic oaths may invite curses)
- rebellion: disregard for laws or for authority which the Bible describes as being instituted by God (Rom. 13:1-7)
- worshiping achievement, education, status, works
- intellectual spirit (a mindset that exalts general knowledge above God's truth and wisdom; it may also manifest when a person tries to give "mental assent" to the Scriptures, just serving out of the intellect, but not walking in power.)
- obsession with wealth
- any obsession that takes most of one's time and mental or emotional energy

IDOLATRY (in fleshly areas)
- gluttony, drunkenness
- addictions: alcoholism, drug or other substance abuse
- lust, impurity, perversions
- adultery
- incest
- homosexuality, lesbianism
- addiction to pornography
- sexual abuse, molestation
- prostitution

DISEASES
- learning disabilities
- retardation
- birth defects

- deformities
- "inherited" diseases such as heart problems, arthritis, cancers, tendency for leukemia, seizures, diabetes, glaucoma, etc.
- spirit of infirmity (this will usually be accompanied by a mindset of infirmity, an expectation of infirmity)

LACK

- low self-esteem
- poverty, fear of lack
- failure
- lack of hope, direction, purpose, motivation

OPPRESSION

- depression, anxiety
- bipolar disorder, manic depression, schizophrenia
- rejection; feelings of inferiority and worthlessness
- compulsive disorders
- confusion
- mental illness
- emotional imbalance
- self-abuse, self-mutilation, self-hatred
- frequent accidents
- suicide
- early death

Sometimes it is easier to identify curses by the behaviors, conditions, and influences which they produce in a home.

Below are two lists. The first consists of signs of demonic work in the environment—*behaviors, conditions, and influences*. The second consists of resulting *mindsets* that can permeate a child's world view despite the best efforts of parents. Remember, the enemy goes about seeking whom he may devour. This truth is found in 1 Peter 5:8: "Be alert and of sober mind. Your enemy the devil prowls around like a roaring lion looking for someone to devour." I believe the devil would like to derail every child while he or she is still too young to realize what is happening. Parents who understand spiritual warfare can put a strong covering over their children. Parents who are ignorant about spiritual warfare lack the tools they need to help defend their own children against generational predators. Positive thinking is good, but spiritual authority is better. Sometimes, despite all the very best efforts of parents, children still go their willful ways.

In adulthood, we must come to an understanding of what has gone on in the spiritual realm if we have been plagued by a struggle. The buck stops with the mature adult. As an adult, I must take a look at my life and take charge of areas that don't match Christ's behavior. By the way, in a home where very bad mistakes have been made while raising children, it is a very healing experience for a child to hear these words from a parent: "I was wrong. Will you please forgive me?"

List #2

Behaviors, Conditions, and Influences Which Often Accompany Generational Curses

(You may wish to add others.)
Everybody makes mistakes. Don't get overwhelmed and feel as if you have to fix thirty or forty areas. I would

put a star beside two or three important culprits and start there. You can always refer to this list later as you are doing routine maintenance on your life. Again, if you really have a lot of issues, believe God for a makeover. People ask for this type of prayer at times in the prayer line in our church; they may say, "I need a Holy Spirit overhaul." God is not limited. This handbook may also assist you in understanding and helping others. A very important point to make here is that not all sins or conditions are generational. Many times people just veer off the good path by their own deliberate choosing.

I want to insert here a story in the Gospels of when Jesus healed a blind man. He said that neither the man nor his parents had sinned. That was not the reason the man was born blind. The man was born blind so that the glory of God could be displayed. Jesus healed the man, and God was glorified. So, even though it sounds as though the man was not under a generational curse, he still had to be healed by the power of God.

When curses have been running in a family, all sorts of behaviors or conditions manifest which are not positive. Below are patterns which do not glorify God. In a way, if a person is laboring under any of these patterns, he is under a type of curse. Jesus came to destroy the works of the devil. Sometimes it's good to see on paper the various forms the enemy's work can take. We don't want to be the devil's helper by perpetuating any of these issues, if we can help it. In the case of disease or poverty, the battle may be long and intense. A working of miracles can bring a sudden deliverance. Most often, breakthroughs are wrought through standing on the Word over time. (Methods of spiritual warfare are presented in chapter 5.)

The issues below can be signals that curses are at work. *These issues may be the result of generational curses; or, they may simply be symptoms of roots that need to be addressed, as in the case of passivity, for example.* I really want to stress that not all the conditions and behaviors listed below are generational curses, but I believe many of these conditions may exist if one has been shaped in an environment where generational strongholds were present. Do not get overly introspective. Just highlight problem areas, consider yourself alerted, and claim the victory.

CONFUSION AND MADNESS

- anger
- rage
- unreasonably hard spankings, physical abuse
- screaming, yelling, throwing things (sometimes at people)
- slapping across the face or hitting impulsively; shoving
- hitting children with objects
- tying children up, locking them in closets, withholding food
- verbal abuse, debasing self or others
- inability to deal with normal frustrations
- road rage
- retaliation
- beatings, cruelty
- violence
- hazing, bullying
- rape
- murder
- bitterness, disappointment
- hatred

- strife
- critical, fault-finding spirit
- arguing; destructive criticism
- gossip, slander
- inability to confront or to address conflict in an open, rational manner
- the silent treatment, inability to move past a hurt
- unresolved conflicts
- lack of affection in the home
- emotional abandonment
- disconnectedness in the home, lack of interaction
- unforgiveness, grudges, feuds
- separation, divorce, abandonment
- gang activity as a substitute for family relationships
- fear
- phobias such as fear of germs, crowds, heights, sounds, lights, etc.
- anxiety: resulting conditions such as ulcers, skin rashes, headaches, asthma, palpitations, etc.
- fear of taking risks, of making decisions, or of taking responsibility
- fear of making mistakes; inertia, inability to move in any direction
- fear of lack; worrying about money

LACK

- a mindset of lack
- low self-esteem, low achievement
- poor spending habits, living on credit or welfare
- poverty, lack of necessities
- shiftlessness, unstable lifestyle, moving frequently (not referring to military or migrant work)
- low expectations for oneself or for one's children

- unemployment, street life, homelessness
- wasting time, laziness, excessive sleeping, drifting
- unreliability, unaccountability

IDOLATRY IN THE FORM OF REBELLION, WHICH IS WITCHCRAFT (1 Sam. 15:23)

- lawlessness
- disrespect for parents (contrary to the fifth commandment)
- disrespect for authority (Romans 13:1-7)
- abortion
- greed
- theft, forgery, other illegal practices
- incarceration
- destruction of public property, arson
- failure to pay fines; disregard for ordinances and various laws
- cheating on taxes, lying to authorities, falsifying documents, forgery, identity theft
- drug manufacturing, drug dealing

IDOLATRY IN THE FORM OF MISPLACED PRIORITIES

- religious spirit; emphasis on form without power; dogmatism; trusting in works
- pride
- obsession with high achievement or greatness; having to prove one's worth
- more emphasis on education than on spiritual oneness with God
- worshiping achievement, education, status, works
- unrealistic expectations for children, pressure on children

- inordinate emphasis on sports, pageants, trophies, having children that must be "number one"
- intellectualism, or an intellectual spirit: a mindset that exalts general knowledge above God's wisdom and truth; excessive dependence on human reasoning
- excessive pride over wealth; obsession with making money
- root-level insecurity about one's God-given worth
- prejudice, discrimination

IDOLATRY AS A CONSCIOUS FORM OF WORSHIP

- idolatry in the form of false religious practices
- the occult: sorcery, witchcraft, astrology; spiritism; consulting mediums; psychic readings, fortune telling, palm reading
- use of horoscopes, Ouija boards, 8-balls, tarot cards, etc.
- cultic rituals, sacrifices, séances
- cultic oaths or incantations (Some seemingly religious groups require oaths which may invite curses.)
- hypnotism (Letting one's will be controlled by another human being can open one up to demonic oppression; we should yield our wills to God only.)

IDOLATRY IN THE FORM OF PUTTING ONE'S FLESH ABOVE GOD'S LAWS

- unrestrained appetite
- overeating, gluttony; excess in self-indulgence
- drunkenness
- abortion, which results when one indulges in pleasure but does not accept responsibility for the consequences
- all types of sexual sin

- lack of personal holiness and self-control; self-gratification
- lust, impurity, perversions
- adultery
- addiction to pornography
- introducing children to sexual activity
- molestation, voyeurism, exhibitionism
- child trafficking
- prostitution
- homosexuality, lesbianism
- incest

OPPRESSION

- depression, anxiety
- nervous ticks
- spirit of regret (continuing to regret past failures or poor choices)
- bipolar disorder, manic depression; schizophrenia
- rejection, feelings of inferiority and worthlessness, low self–image
- relationship addiction (always looking for love, usually in the wrong places)
- insomnia
- passivity: not rising up to rule in one's circumstances (Thompson, pp. 15 and 20)
- inability to initiate action, make decisions, or face responsibilities
- repetitious pastimes: compulsive television watching, video gaming, etc.
- sudden flashes of thought; sudden stoppage of thought; racing thoughts; thoughts dominated by patterns of worry, fear, or rejection (Some thoughts and thought patterns are the work of evil spirits; reject these.)

- lack of concentration
- tendency to leave jobs unfinished, to abandon goals
- eating disorders: anorexia, bulimia, gorging
- compulsive disorders, obsessive-compulsive disorders
- compulsive eating, spending, hoarding, cleaning, etc.
- excessive intake of unhealthful substances such as sugar, caffeine, stimulant foods (self-medicating with food)
- addictive behaviors—use of tobacco, drugs, alcohol, prescription drugs
- self-punishment: unconsciously letting guilt cause physical symptoms such as headaches, stomachaches, and other physical anomalies
- confusion
- mental illness, emotional imbalance
- accident-proneness, recklessness, self-destruction
- self-mutilation, self-punishment, cutting, tattooing
- suicide

DISEASES AND DISORDERS

- learning disabilities
- ADD
- ADHD
- dyslexia and related learning differences
- blindness, deafness, mute aspect
- retardation
- birth defects (Again, be very careful not to take oaths in seemingly "religious" groups.)
- "inherited" tendencies for certain diseases such as heart disease, cancers, leukemia, arthritis, seizures, diabetes, glaucoma, etc.
- early death

Why not take a moment to highlight or list (on Journal page #2) any of these behaviors, conditions, or influences that stand out to you? Remember, you are not going to try to change all behaviors or conditions at once. Face the issues; then pick out one or two key areas that you need to deal with first. Often addressing one issue and getting the victory there will spill over into other areas and produce additional benefits. For example, taking charge of eating habits can produce victory in many other areas of the flesh. Another example: conquering *anxiety* can help relieve many other issues. In fact, conquering anxiety by letting God's peace rule is probably one of the greatest blessings a Christian can choose to exercise.

Disease and poverty usually require some particularly intense warfare. However, if one understands that Jesus paid for these issues, he can doggedly put his faith out for victory and deliverance. I'll say it repeatedly in this book: staying saturated in the Word, confessing the Word, standing on the Word—it cannot be overemphasized. By His stripes we are healed. I recommend memorizing Mark 11:23 where we find that we can speak to any mountain and see it removed.

The difference between the approach in this book and the approach in many rehab environments is that here you are specifically asking God to help you deal with the spiritual roots behind harmful behaviors and conditions. The secular community is usually reluctant to acknowledge that evil spirits still exist and influence people. For some reason, living in modern times gives people the illusion that the spiritual realm has somehow changed since Jesus's days of earthly ministry.

Let me emphasize that often a struggling person is primarily dealing with negative thought patterns which originate with demonic lies. We want to change our think-ing and not accept the oppression that comes with false mindsets. Anything that puts you down, makes you feel "less than," or makes you afraid to live is really from the enemy. Evil spirits can plant negative thoughts. You don't have to receive their thoughts, though. You don't have to accept disease, either. It is easier to accept it than to fight, but it's worth the fight. God is holding out abundant life to us. Demons can't read our minds, but they can watch our actions and hear what we say out of our own mouths. They can learn where we have been vulnerable.

If you are feeling overwhelmed at this point, relax. I believe the testimonies in chapter 7 will show you how God tailor-makes a plan for all who come to him. Each one can learn to rule over his enemies by conquering false mindsets. Getting God's view sets the stage for faith.

If you are currently in any rehab situation, take all that is offered. You can benefit from the support of group discussions. The listening ear of a trained counselor can be a great blessing. Sometimes just hearing yourself talk works wonders. Hearing others talk out their issues can also help one gain a right perspective. Along with every secular rehab opportunity, be aware also of the spiritual side. Take everything Jesus is holding out. A good rule of thumb would be this: use all the tools you can get.

Mindsets and Words Which Often Accompany Negative Patterns or Strongholds

Now we zero in on the realm of thoughts and words. Your subconscious mind actually undergirds your thinking, and mindsets can so permeate your world view that you don't even know they are operating! These mindsets can form the basis for thinking and reacting. We absorb mind-sets from our environment even when we don't know it is happening. It is vital to allow the Holy Spirit to show you on a daily basis from what source your thoughts originate.

If you find that negative tapes are playing in your head, you can cast down these thoughts. Consider the verse below. When you cast down imaginations, you are casting down thoughts and reasonings. If the thoughts going through your mind are destructive, replace them with God's truth as found in the Word. This is what is meant by bringing every thought captive "to the obedience of Christ."

Thinking

"Casting down imaginations, and every high thing that exalteth itself against the knowledge of God, and bringing into captivity every thought to the obedience of Christ." (2 Corinthians 10:5 KJV)

Speaking

"Do not let any unwholesome talk come out of your mouths, but only what is helpful for building others up according to their needs, that it may benefit those who listen." (Ephesians 4:29)

Verbal Witchcraft

Be aware that you have the power of life and death in the tongue. This verse should be coursing through our thoughts every day: "The tongue has the power of life and death, and those who love it will eat its fruit" (Proverbs 18:21). Just imagine what can be brought about if we are saying things like this: so-and-so will never succeed; so-and-so always has problems; so-and-so is a failure. You know, just to play it safe, I plead the blood over myself in case anyone is loosing witchcraft over me through gossip. I do not think I am paranoid, not at all. I hear the way some people talk about others! We should speak well of others, and we should put a covering over ourselves in case they are not speaking well of us. Another sobering thought is that we reap what we sow. We should be talking this way: so-and-so is generous; so-and-so handles money well; so-and-so walks in divine health.

Identifying negative thinking and speaking patterns gets easier with practice. Here is a list of mindsets or words which are not beneficial. Remember, thought patterns can become deeply engrained, producing attitudes and behaviors. We want to bring lies and other harmful thoughts into captivity and replace them with God's Word. God meant for words to build up and edify.

List #3

Mindsets and Words

Remember, truth is our model; we stand on truth.

Faulty Mindsets and Words	God's Truths Showing Us What Is Right
I just hate so-and-so.	Truth: "The fruit of the Spirit is love, joy, peace, patience, kindness, goodness, faithfulness, gentleness, self-control; against such things there is no law." Gal. 5:22-23 (NASB)
It's okay to steal because this big store will never miss this stuff. I'll just help myself to supplies at work. My boss won't know if I'm a few minutes late.	Truth: "Everyone who sins breaks the law; in fact, sin is lawlessness." 1 John 3:4 Truth: "Thou shalt not steal." Exodus 20:15 (KJV)
I don't have to follow these dumb rules.	Truth: "For rebellion is as the sin of witchcraft, and stubbornness is as iniquity and idolatry." 1 Samuel 15:23 (KJV)
We are better than other people.	Truth: "He mocks proud mockers but shows favor to the humble and oppressed." Pr. 3:34
I feel superior. People in our family are more talented and more intelligent than other people.	Truth: "When pride comes, then comes disgrace, but with humility comes wisdom." Pr. 11:2
Money is everything.	Truth: "You cannot serve both God and money." Luke 16:13

If you are not rich, you are a nobody.	Truth: "The LORD does not look at the things people look at. People look at the outward appearance, but the Lord looks at the heart." 1 Samuel 16:7
Education is everything.	Truth: "Knowledge puffs up, while love builds up." 1 Cor. 8:1
Having brains is everything. Being handsome or beautiful physically is everything.	Truth: "The grass withers and the flowers fall, but the word of our God endures forever." Isa. 40:8
We'll never have anything. We will always be poor.	Truth: "And my God will meet all your needs according to the riches of his glory in Christ Jesus." Phil. 4:19
I feel inferior. We are trailer trash.	Truth: "I am fearfully and wonderfully made." Ps. 139:14 (KJV)
I am afraid to try this. I feel intimidated.	Truth: "For God hath not given us the spirit of fear; but of power, and of love, and of a sound mind." 2 Timothy 1:7 (KJV)

Why was I ever born? I wish you had never been born. I wish I had never been born. Why can't you be like your brother? Why can't you be like your sister? I should have been a boy/girl. You are a disappointment. Something is wrong with me. Every family has a black sheep, and I'm it. My kids are losers. I'm a loser. You are a loser. Nothing ever works out for me. It would be easier to be dead. I'll never be anything. Life is hard. Life is bad.	Truth: "Your eyes saw my unformed body; all the days ordained for me were written in your book before one of them came to be." Ps. 139:16 Truth: "I am fearfully and wonderfully made." Ps. 139:14 (KJV) Truth: "The tongue has the power of life and death." Pr. 18:21 Truth: "'For I know the plans I have for you,' declares the Lord, 'plans to prosper you and not to harm you, plans to give you hope and a future.'" Jeremiah 29:11

I'm stupid. I'm a loser.	Truth: "I am fearfully and wonderfully made." Ps. 139:14 (KJV)
I have a learning disability. I'm always in special ed.	Truth: "But we have the mind of Christ." 1 Cor. 2:16
Other people have it easier than I do.	Truth: "In this world, you will have trouble, but take heart! I have overcome the world." John 16:33
I can't handle stress.	Truth: "They go from strength to strength, till each appears before God in Zion." Ps.84:7-8 Truth: "God has not given us a spirit of fear; but of power, and of love, and of a sound mind." 2 Timothy 1:7 (KJV)
People in our family are fat.	Truth: "The fruit of the Spirit is ... self-control." Gal. 5:22, 23
Nobody ever gives me a chance.	Truth: "Knock and the door will be opened to you." Matthew 7:7
You are our pride and joy—all of our hopes are resting on you.	Truth: "... fixing our eyes on Jesus, the pioneer and perfecter of faith." Heb. 12:2

I'm an addict. I just can't get free.	Truth: "No temptation has over-taken you but such as is common to man; and God is faithful, who will not allow you to be tempted beyond what you are able, but with the temptation will provide the way of escape also, so that you will be able to endure it." 1 Cor. 10:13 (NASB)
I'll always be like this. I can never change.	Truth: "I can do all through Christ which strengtheneth me." Phil. 4:13 (KJV)
It would take a miracle for this to be healed, and there's no way I'm going to get a miracle.	Truth: "I am the LORD, the God of all mankind. Is there anything too hard for me?" Jeremiah 32:27
Everyone in our family dies of cancer by age 40. Our family is cursed with overweight. We all get arthritis or glaucoma.	Truth: "By his wounds we are healed." Isa. 53:5
When I find my spouse, then I will be complete. When I have a baby, then I will have someone to love.	Truth: "…and to know this love that surpasses knowledge—that you may be filled to the measure of all the fullness of God." Eph. 3:19

I was born to be gay. I can choose my sexual preference. I can do whatever I want with my body.	Truth: "The wrath of God is being revealed from heaven against all the godlessness and wickedness of men who suppress the truth by their wickedness, since what may be known about God is plain to them, because God has made it plain to them.....Therefore God gave them over in the sinful desires of their hearts to sexual impurity for the degrading of their bodies with one another. They exchanged the truth of God for a lie, and worshiped and served created things rather than the Creator... Because of this, God gave them over to shameful lusts. Even their women exchanged natural relations for unnatural ones. In the same way the men also abandoned natural relations with women and were inflamed with lust for one another. Men committed indecent acts with other men, and received in themselves the due penalty for their perversion." Rom.1:18-19, 24-25a, 26-27 Truth: "Do not lie with a man as one lies with a woman; that is detestable." Lev. 18:22 Truth: "Do you not know that your bodies are temples of the Holy Spirit, who is in you, whom you have received from God? You are not your own; you were bought at a price. Therefore honor God with your bodies." 1 Cor. 6:19-20 Truth: "Do not cut your bodies for the dead or put tattoo marks on yourselves. I am the Lord." Lev. 19:28

I hope you will pause to write down any insights you get as to false mindsets or words that you absorbed growing up. You can jot your insights on page #3 in the Journal section. You can imagine that if a child grew up hearing words from the right column spoken over him/her frequently, and if the home were in balance, there would be great cause for confidence and success in the child. Many children overcome no matter what. I believe God has placed great resilience in children, and that this explains why some children surmount incredible odds.

Finishing your profile

Your Medical Factors and Personality Issues

There may be unique medical issues or personality issues that played into your development. As you continue reading, you may wish to jot down unique medical or personality factors that influenced your development, especially as you read through the four testimonies in chapter 7 (record on Journal p. #4).

A Life Trigger

At this point, you may already be thinking about an event or circumstance in your life that first began to take you on a downhill path, or which caused you to shrink back from challenges. If this is clear in your mind, go ahead and note that on your Journal page. You may already have dealt with that circumstance. Working this aspect through may involve forgiveness—forgiving oneself or forgiving others. (Journal p. #5)

Chapter 4

Three Epidemics Demystified

S oon we will move on to the strategies of shaking off negative patterns. We will also look at giftings and goals. First, however, let's take a closer look at some labels and diagnoses that seem very prevalent today. In fact, the primary reason that I set out to put this book together is that I wanted something to hand to people who tell me they have the conditions that I discuss in this chapter. I want so much to explain to them that they don't have to receive a label or a diagnosis that must become permanent. Frequently, as I minister to women who are in jail, the issues in this chapter come up. If you've gotten one of these labels or diagnoses, just remember that with God all things are possible. Just because a person is in a battle doesn't mean he or she has to accept some permanent label.

Bye-bye, Black Sheep

Why is it that in many families, it seems as if one child has more problems than the others? I have heard it said that there is really no such thing as a black sheep. The rationale is that there can be a child in the family who seems to be sensitive and who absorbs the hurts, disappointments, conflicts, inconsistencies, and pressures of the family. This sensitive child may not know how to process all this negative energy.

This one appears to have all the problems. Actually, often-times he or she is trying to carry the burden of the inconsistencies that are perceived to be in the rest of the family.

Well, the Christian can learn how to deal with all this baggage. Drop it! I felt like a black sheep; maybe you have too. Perhaps you have a God-given sensitivity which the Lord wants to harness to help others. Once a person is healed, he can take that sensitive nature and quit turning it inward on himself; one can turn it outward. It takes a sensitive person to walk in another's shoes. Sensitivity is an attribute which can be shaped for positive use.

Adult Bipolar Disorder

I am including this section for one reason: I have met an army of people who have been labeled "bipolar." It seems to me that this diagnosis is being tossed about in epidemic numbers. A neighbor tells me her daughter is bipolar; a woman in the jail says she is bipolar. What is bipolar?

Bipolar has to do with manic depression, or mood swings. There are plenty of reasons that a person might experience mood swings, but first I am going to present the spiritual side of the bipolar issue. Then I'll present some medical conditions that can also produce mood swings, making a person perhaps appear to be bipolar. Probably there are a number of people who have a severe case of the bipolar syndrome. They may have a diagnosis from a reputable doctor. I'm not saying that people should refuse medication, but I am saying that one should be aware that sometimes what is called "bipolar" is perhaps aggravated by spirits or by an unresolved medical issue. If you are under treatment due to a bipolar diagnosis, continue that treatment as you sort out your root issues and your options.

As we mature and take charge over our personalities, we can find much victory by choice. Personally, I would not lightly receive a bipolar label from anyone. You might just say you are "battling mood swings." Never claim to *be* bipolar. You would just be receiving the enemy's label. You would be labeling yourself as unstable. That's a bad confession. It may be true that you are being treated for the bipolar syndrome, but avoid labeling yourself as *being* bipolar. Confess that you are healed, and keep your tongue lined up with the Word of God.

You may still have symptoms. You confess your healing by faith. This releases power into your situation. When a healing happens suddenly, we call that a miracle. However, many wonderful healings unfold progressively, over time.

Spirits may operate in pairs or in sets

Even people who don't read the Bible much know the story of the demoniac from the Gerasenes (sometimes spelled Gadarenes)—the naked man among the rocks who cut himself and could not be chained. In this Gospel account, Jesus had come across the lake. I am certain He knew that He would see the demoniac because that man must have had quite a reputation. As Jesus approached the rocky place, the demoniac came running and fell at His feet. Now, this looked as if the man wanted to worship Jesus; however, out of his mouth came the words, "What do you want with me, Jesus, Son of the Most High God? I beg you, don't torture me!" (Luke 8:28).

Jesus knew the man had an unclean spirit and had commanded the spirit to come out of him. Jesus asked the spirit its name, and it answered, "Legion," because many demons had gone into the man. Now, I'm not here to talk about "possession" as opposed to "oppression," but I will say that evil spirits often work in sets, or in pairs. As this story goes, Jesus commanded that the spirits go into a herd of pigs. The demons made two thousand pigs crazy, and they ran downhill into the lake and drowned. That was an economic loss for the people of that region. Of course, what were Jews doing with pigs, anyway, since pigs were unclean for the Jews? It looks as if Jesus solved a pig problem and a human problem at the same time. Note that this was not a parable, by the way. It's an account of deliverance.

I don't think I ever had two thousand demons against me, but I used to suffer from manic depression. I do believe the Lord revealed to me the source of this, at least in my case. Sometimes a manic, or driving, spirit would come to harass me. At these times, I would have racing thoughts, bursts of creative energy, and feel as if I were on a high. I didn't really have a lot of patience at those times, and I could feel trapped and want to leave a place, quit a job, or move. At other times, a different spirit would oppress me, a spirit of depression. I would feel hopeless, as if to say, "What's the point in trying?" At times like this, I would feel empty, desolate, lifeless, with no motivation, unable to see five feet ahead, just down. It is possible that my body chemistry may have been out of balance, but I am certain that spirits were also playing a part.

Gradually, I began to grasp that evil spirits were involved. I am not saying that I was possessed by demons. I'm just saying spirits were involved. One day I believe the Lord revealed to me clearly that I was dealing with two spirits which were taking turns coming against my mind and emotions. In a way, they were camouflaging one another, because not just one condition was manifesting. I began to take dominion over these spirits. By that I mean I resisted their influence by taking charge of my moods. What convinced me that the depression and mania were aggravated by the work of evil spirits was that when I would choose to worship God in song, the patterns would leave me.

Here's how I took dominion. When I would feel depressed, I would make myself get going, even when I didn't feel like it. For example, when I was in my thirties, I was very sorry that I was still single. People would ask me to sing at their weddings, and I figured this was God's way of helping me get outside of my own little pity party. I would sing at weddings just to prove to the devil that he wasn't going to keep me down. At other times, when the manic side hit me, I would have racing thoughts or get on some creative streak that felt as if it could last all night. At these times, I would calm myself down and meditate in Scripture until I could sleep. I was able to do this once I understood that I was really being harassed by demon spirits. I didn't have to put up with it. I learned to dislike the enemy enough to resist his tactics. I learned to trust God enough to tenaciously believe He had something good for me down the road. I got control of my moods by deciding to. Understanding the work of spirits made it easier because I realized that I did not really have to accept some permanent psychological imbalance. I realized that I was the boss. It wasn't easy at first, but I took charge.

Creativity and the bipolar issue

You can consult almost any source and find that historians consider many famous creative people to have been bipolar. The list includes artists such as Vincent Van Gogh and Michelangelo. Among writers they usually cite Hans Christian Anderson, Robert Frost, Charles Dickens, and Robert Louis Stevenson, to name a few. Check out composers: Bach, Beethoven, and Tchaikovsky. Even the great statesman Abraham Lincoln has been viewed in retrospect as having struggled with bipolar tendencies. For example, he would generally have a solemn, melancholy demeanor; then, when telling a story, "his eyes would sparkle, all terminating in an unrestrained laugh" (Goodwin, p.88). In the case of Lincoln, he overcame his melancholy side and was a source of stability to all who knew him, even in the heat of war. We can't know with certainty that these geniuses, if alive today, would have a clinical diagnosis of manic depression. However, history has recorded that these people had excited periods that alternated with periods of depression.

I think most people would agree that creativity comes with challenges. In lab studies, the brain activity recorded during a manic high has resembled the brain activity measured during a creativity spurt. I believe that God made creativity to be a blessing. A creative person can learn to recognize when he or she is on a roller coaster and can take charge. God made creativity. God wants to give us the wisdom and discernment to manage the creativity alongside the other basic gifts in life. We can look to Him for balance. God meant for creativity to be a blessing, not a curse.

Medical conditions which can produce bipolar-like mood swings

Be aware that having mood swings doesn't necessarily mean that a person has a deep psychological problem. In her book, *Adult Bipolar Disorders*, Dr. Mitzi Waltz of the United Kingdom's Birmingham University lists the following medical conditions that can cause a person to experience mood swings. You may have been diagnosed as bipolar because of mood swings. However, the mood swings may have more than one cause. There may be various factors aggravating your moods. For me, it was pivotal to discover how low blood sugar affected my moods. When I began limiting sugar and caffeine intake, I experienced more stable blood-sugar levels and a greater sense of well-being. Exercise helps, as does eating fresh fruits and vegetables and protein-rich foods. Intake of excessive starches, sugars, or fats may cause blood sugar swings.

If you suffer from what a doctor has labeled "bipolar disorder," examine this list to see if there might be another condition(s) affecting your moods. I have put an asterisk beside the ones that I believe probably involve the work of mind-hampering spirits. If you want to get technical, all infirmities really involve the work of evil spirits. Jesus healed everyone who came to him. He literally drove off spirits, even when the diseases had been present since birth. If Jesus healed a withered hand or cured eyes by making mud with saliva, just think how He can sooth a confused mind. No condition or combination of conditions is too much for God. Whether a person's mood swings are aggravated by evil spirits, by medical issues, or by both, God is well able to bring a balance as His power works through a renewed mind.

Here is Dr. Waltz's list, composed from the standpoint of a research psychologist. These are various medical conditions which can contribute to mood swings.

- ADHD ("There's a great deal of overlap between ADHD and bipolar." Waltz, p. 46)
- anxiety*
- conduct disorder
- Cushing's disease
- depression*
- diabetes mellitus
- fibromyalgia
- hormonal disorders

- hypoglycemia
- lupus
- medication side effects
- multiple sclerosis
- personality disorders*
- psychosis* (when one is laboring under extreme confusion with altered perceptions)
- rheumatoid arthritis
- substance abuse
- schizophrenia*
- schizoaffective disorder*
- thyroid disorders
- infectious illness
- AIDS
- chronic fatigue syndrome
- hepatitis
- infectious mononucleosis
- seizure disorders

Balancing treatment and prayer

Some of these conditions are psychological, and others are more physical, though there is usually an overlap of both in any condition. Jesus can heal any affliction. I want to stress very clearly here that if you need a doctor's help with therapy and medications, stick with that approach as long as you must. Know this, however: behind any disease, there is a spirit—the spirit of infirmity. The more you saturate yourself in the Word, you will discover that disease doesn't have to be taken lying down, no pun intended. Your faith and your understanding of your authority can grow. Two of the greatest teachers I know on this subject are Kenneth and Gloria Copeland. They have richly blessed the body of Christ by explaining how faith-filled words can literally shape your health, or any other aspect of life.

Let's talk some more about the spirit of infirmity. Look at this account found in Luke's gospel. The understanding that a condition can actually be caused by the work of a *spirit of infirmity* is crucially important because you do have authority over evil spirits. This story involves a woman who was physically bent over.

> "Now He [Jesus] was teaching in one of the synagogues on the Sabbath. And behold, there was a woman who had a spirit of infirmity eighteen years, and was bent over and could in no way raise herself up. But when Jesus saw her, He called her to Him and said to her, "Woman, you are loosed from your infirmity." And He laid His hands on her, and immediately she was made straight, and glorified God." Luke 13:10-13 NKJV

This passage of Scripture illustrates what authority can do. It clearly demonstrates that this woman's bent-over condition, which she had endured for eighteen years, was caused by a spirit. The Greek phrase in verse 10 would translate literally as "having a spirit of illness." In the Greek it reads *pneuma echousa astheneias*. The word *pneuma* means "spirit." The woman was bent over and could not straighten up. When she was loosed from this spirit, she did straighten up. You really have to make a choice when studying the Bible. Are you going to learn about the spiritual realm the way the Bible presents it, or are you going to let your thinking be molded by modern mindsets based on a trust in man's study of medicine alone? Are you going to be afraid of being labeled as foolish, or simply take the Word as it is written?

The time may come when your faith and your understanding of how demonic spirits work will increase; then you may rise up and cast oppressive symptoms down. When that time comes, it is wise to be under spiritual authority, having pastors and/or intercessors in your church praying along with you. Also, if you decide to reduce or stop a medication, it is wise to ask your doctor to monitor your progress. Accountability is a wise path.

If you have to stay under therapy and on medication, there is no condemnation. God takes us where we are. However, just know this: your healing is paid for. I have learned that it usually takes great tenacity to receive certain types of healing—tenacity in the form of spiritual warfare, standing on the Word, and confessing the Word, no matter what the symptoms are. As one of my pastors says, "It is easier to just accept disease than it is to fight. Many people choose not to fight. They may say to God, 'God, if it's your will, heal me. If it's not your will to heal me, I'll carry this sickness for the glory of God.' Guess what! Disease does not glorify God. You can serve Him much better in a healthy state."

I know of people who have read the Bible for years but have never overcome depression. How sad. There really should come a day when this person is able to mix faith with the knowledge of the Word, rise up, and take dominion over the work of the enemy. You do this by stating and standing on what the Word says: "I am healed." We tend to seek doctors first in America, praying last. God is holding out such power to us if only we would use it.

Avoid presumption

Presumption is not faith. Don't throw your crutches into the trash can apart from the unction of God, or just goes off meds because it's easier than taking pills. You want to build up your faith by knowing God's Word and confessing it over yourself. When the faith is there, there is a confidence from God that nothing can stop. If you are in presumption, you will probably not succeed. I would not go off meds without the unction of God. I will tell you later how I went cold turkey off three medications at once; but if I were doing that again, I would let my pastor know so as to get some prayer covering.

Once, in Bible school, we had a guest speaker who got me pumped up regarding healing. I went out to the lobby after the meeting, broke my eyeglasses in two, and threw them in a trash can. After a few days of squinting, my eyes were worn out; so I got another pair. I was in the climate of a Bible school, and I wanted to have big faith as other people seemed to. God heals eyes, but I was not in faith.

We are not to force God, force Him to act. That is why Jesus did not jump off the temple when the devil tempted Him (Matthew 4; Luke 4). The devil said that the angels would catch Jesus, quoting from Psalm 91. Jesus, however, knew it was not God speaking; so He didn't jump. Don't go off the meds unless you actually believe God has given you the faith to do this. (By the way, Jesus had the faith to be safe even if he *did* jump. It's just that Satan was tempting him to get personal glory by some shortcut. Jesus knew that he was going to suffer on the cross, not do stunts.)

To sum up, various medical conditions can contribute to mood swings. Demons can also trigger mood swings. To be entirely accurate, a spirit of infirmity is involved any time there is illness or oppression. If you are on medication and/ or under psychiatric care for a bipolar diagnosis, continue with that until a time may come when your faith surpasses this approach. Truly you can be free, but always follow the peace of God and the wisdom He gives. I recommend being under close pastoral and medical supervision if you decide to change your medical routine. I don't say this because I am a doctor; I am not medically trained. However, I have walked with God and have learned some lessons the hard way. Let the peace of God rule. God is a father, a "family man," so to speak. He doesn't want his children wandering around confused. Choose a spiritual mentor to assist you in decisions. If you desire to change your treatment, be accountable to your physician and to your pastor. Be under a spiritual covering. God, in his mercy, has put able people here to help us all.

Seek first the kingdom of God

Now for a word about spiritual disciplines when you are coming out of oppression. Whether or not you are currently institutionalized, take advantage of every spiritual resource at your fingertips—church, chapel, godly counsel, Bible reading, Christian books, sharing your faith with those around you, praying at all times. Exercise in any way you can, and eat the best diet possible. As God renews your mind, you want to feel your best. We know that exercise releases chemicals in the body that produce a sense of well-being. Don't sit and think all the time. Share your faith. Move about.

Some women in jail have shared with me concrete ways in which they express their faith while they are doing jail time. One girl said she helps three types of people with their cleaning chores: women over fifty, pregnant women, and women who are detoxing. Another inmate told me she leads a prayer circle in her tank. Some ladies do each other's hair, or they share hygiene products with those who lack the funds to buy commissary items. One reads aloud to cell mates from a daily devotional or from Scripture. Another might listen while a cell mate unloads. At times, the best witness is just to refrain from getting caught up in the strife that can occur in close quarters. If women in jail can find ways to minister, we all can. Seeking God's kingdom, or souls, and His righteousness is part of the path to healing, no matter where you are.

Church attendance

If you are able to attend church, choose a "power" church. By that I mean, choose a church where the gifts are in operation. This will be a church where there is room in the church service for God to move. I cannot stress this enough. Some examples are these: prophetic utterances may occur in an orderly manner, the pastors may feel they are to form a prayer line during the service, people may get saved or filled with the Spirit or healed in the prayer line, someone may have a word of knowledge about a healing God is doing, or someone may have a spiritual song. If you are in a church, ask yourself if there is room in the services for the Holy Spirit to move when His presence enters. If there is no flexibility in the services for a move of God, why would you stay in such a fellowship? If you are institutionalized and attending the chapel provided, believe God to touch you no matter what the order of worship is. Jesus said, "For where two or three are gathered together in my name, there am I in the midst of them" (Matthew 18:20 KJV).

Schizophrenia

In this section, I address schizophrenia from a spiritual standpoint. I meet so many people who tell me they have been diagnosed as schizophrenic. It's time to expand a public awareness that this disorder can be relieved, not just treated with medication. I have borrowed, by permission, from the work of Dr. Carroll Thompson, long-time instructor at Christ for the Nations Institute in Dallas, Texas. His discussion of schizophrenia is presented in his teaching series, *Possess the Land*, and is available on tape and in print.

Schizophrenia from a spiritual standpoint

Dr. Thompson asserts that the secular community discusses schizophrenia from a purely medical standpoint, describing it usually in terms of chemical imbalances, certain observable behaviors, and perceptual abnormalities, such as hearing voices. Dr. Thompson believes that the medical community describes mostly the symptoms of schizophrenia, but not the roots. Often medicine is prescribed to help people cope, but medicine does not get at the roots. Counseling can bring some understanding, but deliverance comes through the power of God. Even then, it will take concerted effort to re-pattern one's thinking and behaving.

Let's discuss a couple of phenomena that may occur for a person struggling with schizophrenia. When describing the phenomenon of hearing voices, the medical community uses the term "auditory hallucinations." I will tell you that I once heard a demon speak out loud. I had backslidden, and a demon was expressing the fact that he was glad. This experience straightened me right up. I can promise you that most professionals will laugh at you if you mention that demons can speak out loud. I am sure there are some Christian psychiatrists who know this fact, but I think such doctors are hard to find. I am not down on doctors. Doctors can really help people. I will state clearly, though, that if you rely one hundred percent on secular psychiatrists' views, you will miss the powerful truth that mental disorders involve demonic activity. Don't ever let the word "demonic" frighten you, because Jesus has already given us absolute authority over every such influence.

As for altered visual perceptions, I experienced that too. When I was at my peak point of stress, some things did not look totally real, such as trees or stop signs. For a while, tall, vertical objects sometimes looked like props. Once I got down to the roots of my stress and received God's new direction, these altered perceptions ceased. Initially, I did stabilize with the help of medications, but I was able to stop using medications after about three months. I will add, though, that I had already memorized a lot of Word and was meditating in and confessing what the Word says about healing and peace.

It can be very unnerving to go day after day with altered perceptions. It is especially sad when children hear voices and experience torment. I assure you what they need is deliverance, not just medicine. However, if my child were hearing voices, I would probably get him/her the best medical help possible until we could get our spiritual weapons sharpened. We don't practice our faith on children. We can practice our faith on ourselves, but with children we need to get them under the medical care they need, and pray. We can pray more effectively when we know the doctor's diagnosis. It is important to get the child stabilized medically so that the spiritual side can be addressed. Things may take time.

Roots in the Land

If you have been diagnosed as schizophrenic, relax. There can be some very plausible roots at the bottom of this. Roots can be pulled out when we possess any land. Just as Joshua possessed the land of Canaan, so we must possess the spiritual land God has given us. I like to think that the mind is the inner land. The outer land is made up of souls and territories that God has assigned to us, the fabric of our future. To take the outer land, one must first take the inner land of the mind.

Some of the roots that can make the land difficult to plow are the roots of rebellion, rejection, pride, and the occult, to name a few. Here we will address rebellion and rejection. This discussion of rebellion and rejection stems from the teaching of Dr. Carroll Thompson in his teaching series entitled *Posses the Land*. These two spiritual roots are at the core of what the medical community calls "schizophrenia," or "split personality." Dr. Thompson has graciously given me permission to discuss his insights here.

Rebellion and rejection

The Bible gives some strong words about rebellion. Here is a story which reveals God's view of this root. Early in King Saul's reign over Israel, the prophet Samuel had told Saul to wait for his arrival so the prophet could offer a sacrifice before the army went into battle. Samuel did not arrive as soon as Saul had hoped, so Saul offered a sacrifice on his own, hoping to get into the battle more quickly. Samuel came and announced that this act had doomed Saul's kingship.

Later, Saul was told to destroy the Amalekites and all the plunder. Saul killed most of the Amalekites, but he captured King Agag alive and also kept some of the best livestock. When Samuel arrived and heard the bleating of the sheep, he corrected Saul for disobeying again, saying, "For rebellion is as the sin of witchcraft, and stubbornness is as iniquity and idolatry. Because thou hast rejected the word of the LORD, he hath also rejected thee from being king" (1 Samuel 15:23 KJV).

At the end of Saul's life, he had so grieved the Holy Spirit that he could no longer discern the voice of the Lord. To get direction concerning a battle, he consulted a medium, hoping to conjure up the spirit of Samuel, who was by this time deceased. Sorcery is definitely not on God's list of options. Saul's life progressed from bad to worse. When Saul died in battle, David mourned the loss, having recognized the original seeds of greatness in Saul.

Most of us are not likely to affect a whole nation with an act of rebellion, but through this story we see how God views rebellion. It is "as the sin of witchcraft." We do our children no favor if we ignore rebellion in them. We do ourselves no favor if we continue in rebellion. You can see from this list that hurt in a child can lead to rebellion. Dr Thompson lists the steps to rebellion as follows:

(1) Hurt to resentment
(2) Resentment to bitterness
(3) Bitterness to hatred
(4) Hatred to rebellion (Thompson, p. 37)

Look over these behaviors that can manifest when one suffers from a root of rebellion.
- hatred, violence, murder
- bitterness and unforgiveness
- control, possessiveness, witchcraft
- being self-willed, unteachable, proud
- self-delusion, being self-deceptive
- perversion (Thompson, p. 38)

Now for a look at *rejection*. Rejection can enter a child even in the womb. Sometimes a baby comes unwanted, or the gender of the baby is not what the parent(s) had hoped for. An immature parent may not know how to correct these attitudes, which can then affect the environment for the child. If a child grows up in a home where divorce takes place, a parent dies, or a parent leaves, the abandonment that the child experiences can be interpreted as rejection. Teasing and shaming can bring a sense of rejection and worthlessness, as can a lack of love and affection. Rejection may be at the root of these behaviors:

- loneliness, timidity, shyness
- self-pity
- fantasy
- lust
- insecurity
- negative self-image, self-rejection, self-hatred
- fear of [more] rejection
- jealousy, envy
- depression and suicide (Thompson, p. 38)

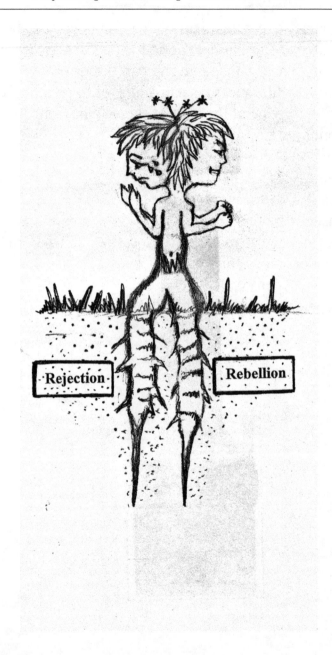

The duality

The person suffering from rebellion will often show outwardly-destructive behaviors. The person suffering from rejection will often show inwardly-destructive behaviors. The person harboring both of these roots, rebellion and rejection, may exhibit alternating behaviors. Schizophrenia, which is a double personality (literally "split mind"), manifests when a person swings from one extreme to the other. First one may be hostile, then withdrawn. The person may lose his real identity and "hide behind one root or the other". Dr. Thompson explains that deliverance involves "treating the two roots" plus bringing the person into "identity with Christ," who becomes his covering. "Finding identity is the key to maintaining deliverance" (Thompson, pp. 38-39).

If this discussion seems to pertain to you, why not begin to put this out before the Lord and apply the attributes of Christ to your self-concept? Begin to identify with Jesus. For a familiarity with what Jesus is like, soak yourself in the four Gospels. If at all possible, present your concerns before a spiritual leader who can pray with you, hopefully one who understands spiritual authority. Also, you can receive much deliverance directly from the Lord. Remember, there is power in the blood and in the name of Jesus. Rather than becoming overly introspective, begin to saturate your mind in the Word of God. I recommend especially Psalms, Proverbs, Matthew, Mark, Luke, John, Ephesians, and Colossians.

The Psalms are like prayers. Proverbs give wisdom. In the four Gospels, you walk the roads with Jesus and experience how he handled oppressed people. You see His great love and His dominion over every affliction. In Ephesians and Colossians, you read of the authority Jesus Christ gives you.

To identify with Christ means to hold Him up as your example. Also, you can picture Christ on the cross bearing all mental torment for you. As you focus on Christ and believe God for the grace to imitate Him, He gives you a point of reference. Jesus said, "I am the way, the truth, and the life" (John 14:6 KJV). Jesus is your equilibrium, literally. Your own thought patterns, focused on Christ, can change. As you read the Word, you will see the blueprint for correct thinking and behavior. Aim for the Bible version of "normal". Jesus is your example. Isaiah 26:3 (KJV) says it this way: "Thou wilt keep him in perfect peace, whose mind is stayed on thee: because he trusteth in Thee."

What if you are on medication for schizophrenia?

Maybe you are on medication right now for schizophrenia. Continue with your medication. Just be aware that understanding can come to you as you immerse yourself in the Word of God. Also, power will enter your spirit. You can begin to recognize the various hurts, bitternesses, or fears from your past. These insights can come to you even as you undergo your regular treatment. Seldom should a person reduce or stop treatment without close medical supervision.

If insights come to you as you study this section, jot them down on Journal pages 1, 2, or 3 at the back of this book. The Holy Spirit, your Comforter and Counselor, can help you gain tremendous insight into the spiritual aspect of any symptoms. Never underestimate the role that the Holy Spirit wants to play in your healing. Inner healing can begin even while a person is on medication or under other forms of therapy.

The battle is not for you only

When I go through a period of intense warfare, I usually end up sharing with others what I am learning. I know that I am not battling for my freedom only, but I am battling also for the people to whom God will assign me. When I battled clinical depression, I often realized that the battle I was fighting was for others also. I knew that this was one of the reasons that the battle was so acute. Somehow I sensed that there would be people in my future that might be helped if I could survive. Here I am, years later, very much wanting to help others. That is the only motive I have for sharing about my weaknesses and past failures. God will assign you to help others, and you will be ready because of what you are learning now.

Jesus is a physician who can pull up the roots with His healing hand. He can cause fruit to thrive in soil which formerly saw only thorns and thistles: "With God all things are possible" (Matthew 19:26 KJV). Nothing cures unbelief like soaking up the Word and confessing it. As you immerse yourself in God's truth, your mind will be renewed. As you gain clarity, you will see through the negative mindsets you have experienced for so long. You will begin to identify them and renounce them. Freedom may be a process; it was for me. If you are in secular counseling and/or are taking medicine, this does not prevent God's Holy Spirit from revealing to you the keys to your own healing. Stay with the counseling and medication as long as you think it best. Remember, "Therefore, there is now no condemnation for them which are in Christ Jesus" (Romans 8:1 KJV). There is a plan for your life, and you will be a blessing to others.

Chapter 5

Shedding the Weights

Whew! We've been looking at a lot of afflictions. It's going to feel good to get on with the victory side. You don't have to put up with sins, negative labels, and curses; but to break them you must do spiritual warfare. An effective method can be to simply renounce evil spirits out loud. I once said out loud, "I renounce bitterness." I felt a strong fluttering motion in my chest, and then it went up and out. I knew that I had cast out a spirit (meaning that I told it to go, out loud, with authority). It had taken root and had been in me a long time. I felt it leave, and I felt different when it had left. I was a Spirit-filled Christian at the time. However, this book is not about casting out. I just want to stress the fact that God can lead you in how to pray and that you have authority.

Much of the time, you are not probably going to see a demon leave, or feel a physical sensation. People who are seasoned in deliverance do frequently see into the spiritual realm and watch spirits leave others. The seeing part is definitely not something to seek after. The deliverance itself is worth fighting for and is ours for the taking.

Whether you call it a *spirit* or a *curse*, you want to command oppression to go. I am not here to discuss demon *possession*, but I think we can all recognize demonic *oppression*. Great power is released when you command, with your own mouth, that oppression must go. You can name a specific spirit such as *bitterness, addiction, anger, lust, pornography*, etc., and command it to go. Do it out loud. Keep standing. Having done all, stand. Keep confessing that the power of it is broken. Keep thanking God for the victory. Sing praise to God, thanking Him for the victory. Hearing yourself praise God for your own victory causes faith to rise in you. "So then faith cometh by hearing, and hearing by the word of God" (Romans 10:17 KJV).

There are many ways to pray. It is not a system of legalistic formulas. God loves us and wants us to succeed. I believe God meets us right where our faith is. He wants us to practice exerting our faith. All through the Bible, God encourages us to be tenacious and to come to him in faith. Flex your faith muscles and pray like you mean it. The more you pray, believing, the greater will be your own faith when you pray. There are many ways to exercise authority. God has given us all the tools we need. Paul said this in Ephesians 1:3: "Praise be to the God and Father of our Lord Jesus Christ, who has blessed us in the heavenly realms with every spiritual blessing in Christ." When God says he has blessed us "with every spiritual blessing," I take that to mean that we are well equipped for every situation.

Let me repeat what my pastor often stresses. When dealing with a long-standing illness or with poverty, one may have to do very intense or prolonged spiritual warfare. It is always easier to just accept circumstances than to fight. However, we have powerful tools.

Let's reflect for just a moment on that pupa in the cocoon. It burns up half its body weight during metamorphosis. As we are energized by the Holy Spirit, taking advantage of these tools that are described in the Word, we too can cast off weights and be transformed for flight. As we become more and more free, all that energy we once used to nurse our habits and wounds will be available to invest in worshiping God and in serving others. We can go from munching leaves on the ground to sipping nectar during flight.

Ten Ways to Rule over Sin and Oppression

1. Command

You can tell a spirit to leave you in the name of Jesus. The name of Jesus is above every name that can be named, as we discussed above (Ephesians 1:18-23). Break the curse in the name of Jesus.

Sometimes when I'm praying for women in the jail, I look right at their faces and command a spirit of addiction or torment to loose them. Some of them are so desperate for freedom that they look me right in the eyes. When I speak the words of deliverance in Jesus's name, it is common for tears to stream from their eyes. Something is broken off, and they know it. They are relieved that someone is willing to help them drive off the spirits that are at the root of the patterns. It is important that the person be ready, sincere, and involved.

A word to the wise: You do have the flesh to deal with. Some habits in our lives are simply the result of our not exercising the self-control God gives us. We can rise up and choose to rule.

2. Renounce

Renounce (out loud) any sinful thought patterns or behaviors that you have allowed to take hold in your life.

An example: "Dear God, I repent for the sin of lust. I renounce lust as a way of thinking. I thank you to cleanse me right now. Thank you, Lord, that it is done."

You can also renounce a pattern. Here is a prayer I once prayed over myself: "Father, I confess that I have never been satisfied with anything I have done. I renounce this way of thinking. I receive the grace to be content with who I am and what I do." If the negative feelings come back, don't let it throw you. Stand. Thank God for his freedom.

If you have ever taken unscriptural oaths in some seemingly "religious" group, be sure to renounce any such oaths. Have no fear. The blood of Jesus covers you, and you have God's backing when you renounce ungodly oaths. Avoid oaths and inner vows. Just stand on the Word of God one day at a time.

3. Plead the blood

You can "plead the blood of Jesus" over yourself, drawing on the power in the blood. Keep thanking God for the power that is in the blood. Demons cannot stand to hear about the blood of Jesus. The mention of it drives them away.

Example: "Dear Heavenly Father, I plead the blood of Jesus over my mind right now. I thank you that the spirit of addiction is broken off my life. I don't want it. I thank you for setting me free by the power that is in the blood of Jesus. I praise you, Lord. I thank you for the power in the blood that Jesus shed for me."

Or, "Father, I thank you that Jesus paid for my healing with His blood. I thank you for my healing. I receive it now and will continue to stand."

4. Resist

> The Word says, "Submit yourselves, then, to God.
> Resist the devil, and he will flee from you" (James
> 4:7). Many times you just stand firm and resist
> the work of the enemy. If you have countered the
> work of the enemy with your words, but the feel-
> ings aren't lining up, do not be thrown off. Just
> keep resisting the pressure that the enemy seems to
> exert against your mind. Remember, the devil, and
> little demonic spirits that work in the hierarchy,
> are powerless to make you do anything. Having
> done all, stand. Jesus is with you: "The one who is
> in you is greater than the one who is in the world"
> (1 John 4:4).

Sometimes oppression comes in the form of thoughts,
especially thoughts which seem to be yours but which actually originate from outside your mind. If your mind has
become somewhat passive, you might not be accustomed
to recognizing the source of thoughts. Are your thoughts
from a book, from your memory, from God, or from evil
spirits? You can spot thoughts that come from evil spirits
because these thoughts will be ungodly or negative, invad-
ing from the outside. Some examples of thoughts (often
carrying emotion) which are prompted by evil spirits
are fear, dread, confusion, panic, or nonsensical notions.
Such thoughts will sometimes "force, push, and coerce
man to take action immediately" (Thompson, p.14). Also,
thoughts coming from evil spirits can "confuse and para-
lyze a man's mind so that it can no longer think clearly."
(Watchman Nee, *The Spiritual Man*) If you encounter
negative thoughts that put you down, evil thoughts that

accuse you or others, or coercive thoughts that seem to push you to act without thinking things through, resist all such thoughts. They are probably demonic in nature.

5. Pray the prayer of agreement

You can pray with another believer, praying in the power of agreement. "Again, truly I tell you that if two of you on earth agree about anything they ask for, it will be done for them by my Father in heaven" (Jesus speaking, Matthew 18:19).

Getting at least two together to agree on a petition multiplies faith.

6. Confess

Concerning physical healing, you can claim your healing on the basis of Scripture. Be tenacious. Isaiah 53:5 and 1 Peter 2:24 are well worth memorizing, meditating on, and confessing. The last part of this verse in 1 Peter is actually a quote from the last part of the verse in Isaiah.

> "But he was pierced for our transgressions,
> he was crushed for our iniquities;
> the punishment that brought us peace was on him,
> and by his wounds we are healed." Isaiah 53:5

"'He himself bore our sins' in his body on the cross, so that we might die to sins and live for righteousness; 'by his wounds you have been healed.'" 1 Per. 2:24

You can confess any truth or Scripture out loud. If you are battling temptation, you can declare you are free, or confess a Scripture that affirms your freedom, such as 1 Corinthians 10:13, which tells us that no temptation is too great for us.

7. Pray in tongues

If you are not sure how to pray, you might want to pray in tongues first. Then pray in English as God gives you His leading. He may bring up a memory. Commit this memory to Him and forgive anyone whom He brings to mind. Unforgiveness can stop the flow of God. If you have not yet exercised tongues (your prayer language), see the "Helps" section, part 2.

8. Praise

Praise is a powerful spiritual weapon. I sometimes just open my Bible up to the Psalms, especially around Psalm 95 through 105, and sing them. On Sunday mornings before church, I like to read Psalm 145 through 150. It can be done anytime. When you are proclaiming God's greatness, you have no idea what victories are being accomplished in the heavenly realm. It's hard to stay depressed when your mouth is praising God. Your heart will catch up.

Here are several gems from the classic *Prison to Praise* by Merlin Carothers.

"The very act of praise releases the power of God into a set of circumstances and enables God to change them if this is His design" (Carothers, p. 91).

"I have come to believe that the prayer of praise is the highest form of communion with God, and one that releases a great deal of power into our lives" (Carothers, p. 92).

"...praise [is] not just a form of worship or prayer, but also a way of waging spiritual warfare" (Carothers, p. 96).

9. Seek counsel or write a letter

If you feel you need prayer, and you are free to travel about (not currently in an institution), seek out mature spiritual counsel with pastoral leaders who know how to operate in the gifts of the Spirit as found in 1 Corinthians chapter 12. If that is not possible, write a letter to a mentor you trust and ask for prayer.

10. Stand

Once you have prayed, stand on the truth that God has undertaken for you. Do not be sin-conscious; rather, be victory-conscious. We do not live in the realm of feelings. If we have done business with God, it will stand. Every day that you stand, the enemy's attempts to bring doubt will grow weaker and weaker, until he gives up. You have far more stamina in battle than the enemy because you have the greater one in you. You are not battling in your own strength alone.

Here is a truth that affirms that God hears our prayers and backs us up: "This is the confidence we have in approaching God: that if we ask anything according to his will, he hears us. And if we know that he hears us—whatever we ask—we know that we have what we asked of him" (1 John 5:14—15). Anytime you are believing God to help you overcome sin or shed some generational weight, you can be confident that you are praying according to his will and that His grace is available.

As you record your prayers on the 6th page of your journal, realize that it is better to focus on one, or maybe two issues at once. Begin with the most pressing. Remember, spiritual warfare is normal for a Christian. As long as we live in this world, we will be engaged in the battle. We take heart knowing that Jesus has overcome the world and has given us victory for the taking.

Chapter 6

Gifts

A Look at the Positive Side

Now we stop to smell the roses. Let's take a breather and consider some blessings and talents God has given us, even if those talents have not yet been developed. Let's stop to remind ourselves about the variety of unique gifts which God has set in motion in our bloodlines. These are the things the devil is after. First, he wants the soul. Then, he would seek to derail a person in life. However, he knows he has no authority; so he tries to keep us in ignorance as to *our* authority. You can beat him on that one by soaking your mind in the Word and confessing it.

You have talents that can be used for God's glory in order to help others. You are a gold mine of potential waiting to be developed and used, and age has nothing to do with it. Below are some gifts that may be itching to find expression. They can all be used to expand the kingdom of God and to improve the world, as God leads. Please mark the gifts that pertain to you, and add any that you think are missing. Some gifts are motivational gifts—gifts that really make us tick. We are pausing here to reflect on the vast creativity and beauty that God has put in us. God really wants us to think on the excellent aspects of life.

The real you is a person who fulfills his/her God-given gifts. Abundant living is creative, godly living.

Keep in mind when looking at gifts that the greatest gift you will ever develop is the anointing of God. When you walk in the anointing, God can anoint and enhance every other gift, making you a truly effective person in the earth. Walking in holiness is a must when cultivating the anointing.

List #4

Gifts

(Please add to the list.)
Circle the ones that speak to you (see Journal page #7).
Remember, gifts can be developed.

- the "five-fold" gifts—apostles, prophets, evangelists, pastors, teachers (Ephesians 4:11) Not everyone is called to the five-fold ministry, but anyone can operate in the gifts of the Holy Spirit.
- the gifts of the Spirit as listed in 1 Corinthians 12:7-11 (KJV) (God's Seven-Eleven):

"But the manifestation of the Spirit is given to every man to profit withal. For to one is given by the Spirit the word of wisdom; to another the word of knowledge by the same Spirit; To another faith by the same Spirit; to another the gifts of healing by the same Spirit; To another the working of miracles; to another prophecy; to another discerning of spirits; to another *divers* kinds of tongues; to another the interpretation of tongues: But all these worketh that one and the selfsame Spirit, dividing to every man severally as he will."

The spiritual gifts listed above are given to willing vessels to bless others, as occasions arise. All the glory goes to God.

- motivational gifts in the Bible—Check out these motivational gifts in Romans 12:6-8.

We have different gifts, according to the grace given to each of us. If your gift is prophesying, then prophesy in accordance with your faith; if it is serving, then serve; if it is teaching, then teach; if it is to encourage, then give encouragement; if it is giving, then give generously; if it is to lead, do it diligently; if it is to show mercy, do it cheerfully.

- praying for people, groups, cities, regions, or nations
- paymaster: one who gives liberally into the kingdom of God
- sales (People who excel at sales often make great soul winners.)
- support skills: keeping the church clean, planting flowers, cutting grass, running sound, CD or tape duplication, greeting, visiting shut-ins
- the gifts of parenting and grand parenting
- all kinds of artistic abilities: painting, sculpting, drawing, architectural design, music, photography
- dance, drama, entertainment that brings people joy and relaxation
- composition gifts: creating works of art in every genre by inspiration and hard work
- writing ability: books, journalism, poetry, songs, letters
- broadcasting
- teaching gifts: school teaching, teaching the Word, assisting in continuing education

- the grace to serve in missions or to assist hurting people groups
- generosity—the ability to give time, money, encouragement
- hospitality; culinary skills
- humor, cheerfulness, people skills, magnetic qualities
- social work; helping people with special needs
- ability to make people feel good about themselves, to be a friend, to be a listener
- mentoring gifts
- ability to counsel
- grace to be a public servant
- generosity in sharing prosperity with those less fortunate

- ability to organize; accounting gifts
- administration, leadership, influence
- legal gifts, the ability to mitigate in a quarrel
- a knack for politics, skills in improving legislature and laws
- ambassadorship; the ability to negotiate or promote peace

- abstract abilities, such as intuition
- ability to grow plants, to farm, to harness nature for man
- ingenuity; a gift for solving problems such as global warming, energy production, protection of the species, protection of our air and water, food production
- abilities in math and the sciences
- the healing arts, doctoring, nursing, nurturing, helping the old or very young
- curiosity to discover new cures or methods

- research gifts in designing health equipment such as for breathing, heart regulation, or dialysis
- technological ability to design defense systems, satellites, farming innovations
- ability to design useful gadgets—phones, computers, cameras, etc.

- physical strength to build roads, bridges, and buildings
- courage to be in law enforcement or corrections
- willingness to serve in the armed forces

- caring for sick or abandoned animals

The list is endless because we are all unique. Our goal is to have a forward mindset, no longer receiving the mindset of limitation. In traditional educational settings, many of our giftings may not have been measured or reinforced. Many people barely survive school, only to find out later in life that they really do have talents. The truth is that every person on this earth has special gifts, in a unique combination that no one else can imitate. You are unique for a reason. Why not jot down gifts you know you possess, as well as gifts you would like to develop?

Setting Goals

Life is, after all, a journey. You wouldn't take a trip without having an itinerary. For the Christian, there must always be a balance when setting goals. I may set goals today, and then God may redirect my path later, making it necessary for me to adjust my plans. However, to have no goals at all is like being a ship at sea with no destination. A good definition of passivity would be this: thinking whatever thought comes to me and drifting in whatever direction life pushes me. We are not called to be passive. We are to take the land. We are to become all God wants us to be.

When setting goals, it's good to set both short-term and long-term goals. A short-term goal might be losing weight, taking a class, starting lessons, or making a resolution. A long-term goal might be a five-year or ten-year goal, such as getting a license or degree, starting a business, or getting a new career. A person might set a goal to improve a relationship with a child or with a spouse. For a long time in my early adulthood, I just went in whatever direction was interesting. Eventually, I came to the point where I had to blend the leading of the Holy Spirit with my own personal goal setting. God would point me in a general direction, but I had to activate my faith by setting concrete goals and sticking with them.

You can stand on Jeremiah 29:11 in which the Lord promises you that He has a future for you, one filled with hope. Even if you have to take your goals on in slow steps, do not let discouragement sway you. You have nothing to lose. You might as well aim high. As you read through the testimonials in the next chapter, think about your own goals and enter your thoughts on page #9 of your journal pages.

Chapter 7

Case Studies
Four Valleys, Four Victories

Ahead lie four valleys. Perhaps you are now journey-ing in one or more of these valleys. In Psalm 139:8-12, God assures us that no matter how low we go, even to the "depths," God is with us. Here are the testimonies of four people who proved this truth, allowing God to rescue them from the mire. They will pinpoint the generational patterns that affected them and the choices they made to walk in freedom. If they did it, so can you. As you read about their "steps to change", you may want to list your own on page #8 of your journal.

A Nervous Breakdown

Carol

The Crash

"All thy waves and thy billows are gone over me."
Psalm 42:7 (KJV)

I stood at the window in my private room in the psychiatric ward at the V.A. Hospital in Dallas, Texas. The metal mesh-work embedded in the window glass on the fourth floor made me wonder if people had tried to jump out. I thought, *Here I am in a mental ward. What is wrong with me? Why do I need medicine in order to relax?* My beige and white, pinstriped pajamas were too short, reminding me of my uniform in the army when nothing had fit quite right due to my height. I thought back over my life. I had been raised by loving parents, gone to college, travelled, become a Christian, come out of the moral pits, gone to Bible school, and tried my hand at Bible translation classes. I could not quite figure out what was wrong. One thing was certain—I needed a rest. Life was straight uphill. Why wasn't it working? Surely by the age of thirty one should be happy and successful.

Just days earlier, I had been studying Bible translation subjects at Wycliffe's Summer Institute of Linguistics in Dallas, Texas. I wasn't sure what I wanted in life, but for now the GI Bill would pay for the classes and my living expenses. Another reason I had chosen translation was that it was the most grand and intellectual thing I could think of to "do for God". I was pretty good at learning languages. I had other abilities, but they didn't seem very important. I reasoned that Bible translation would be the noblest way to spend my life. I reasoned that if I chose a difficult, academic path, this would surely please God. I had been a Christian for five years, having turned from a life of sin and aimless wandering. I had attended two years of Bible school; now it was time to *do something great for God.* I was drawn to music also; but since I didn't read music well, I ruled this out as a career.

Academically, I had been doing fine in my linguistics classes. There was one catch. I had not been able to relax. I was anxious all the time. Trying to relax, I would fast most of the time, eating just two or three small bites at a meal, just enough to keep from starving. Also, I took long walks, trying to unwind. At first the walks lasted about two hours, then longer.

One day, on one of my walks, I had seen a fairly large black snake slither across the path before me. I wondered if it was Satan himself or just a black snake. I realized that to be thinking this way I must be in an altered spiritual state due to too much fasting. I knew that fasts can open a person up to the spiritual realm, and that one should guard against demonic suggestion. I had already been through two years of Bible school, so I knew in principle how things should be. I should feel God's peace. I kept trying to feel that peace.

I would attend linguistic classes, do my homework, then put earphones on and listen to Christian music by the hour. I didn't interact with my roommates or engage in conversation at meals. Everyone else was chattering enthusiastically about linguistics or translation work. I saw that I was withdrawing completely, but I couldn't help it. I had to calm my nerves somehow. Most of the other students were excited about going on the field. I was afraid to go on the field as a single person. As much as I wanted to serve God as a translator, I did not have His peace.

A toxic, subconscious root demands attention

Like a black dart across my soul, a strong temptation badgered me to run, to just go downtown in Dallas and find a man. I had not experienced temptation like that in five years. I knew that some root must be festering in me, some deep root that had not been dealt with. Somehow the pressure of school was bringing this root to the surface. I knew that this tormented soul was not the real me. I had no intention of returning to the worldliness from which God had delivered me, but resisting it took everything.

To complicate matters, a Wycliffe administrator called me into his office and said that if I was going to be a Wycliffe missionary, it was time to apply for member- ship, raise support, and get on with the commitment. He stressed that at age thirty, I wasn't getting any younger. I did not feel ready to make a commitment, knowing that I would have to go on the field as a single person.

A few days before entering the hospital, I had been walk- ing from the dorm to the dining hall on the Bible translation campus. The sidewalk had a slightly uphill grade. I ran out of strength, just standing there on the sidewalk, weak and dizzy. I had fasted so much and taken so many walks that I was completely out of strength. Thinking about it now, I guess it is a miracle that my potassium level hadn't bottomed out. I knew in that moment that I had pushed myself in this direction as far as I could. It was not working. I was at the end of my energy, the end of all physical and emotional strength. I stood there hoping no one was staring at me. I waited, not sure how God would get me out of this one.

On my walks, I had noticed a friendly-looking little cottage on the other side of the Wycliffe property with a sign that read "Counseling Office." I decided to try to walk across the highway to that part of the campus. I had to zigzag across a large parking lot to avoid an uphill incline. Walking slowly and deliberately to avoid fainting, I crossed the highway and entered the counseling center. I said to the receptionist, "I think I need counseling." I was crumbling. I could barely speak without breaking down in tears. I felt very embarrassed and self-conscious about this inability to hide my emotions. I felt very weak physically.

Soon I was talking to Harry Bascom, a Wycliffe counselor who helped translation people work through psychological struggles. "You could join a group therapy session on a weekly basis with other students," he suggested.

"You don't understand. I'm too weak to walk across the road," I answered feebly.

Very soon, he decided to let me stay at his home, which was close by in Duncanville. I tried to sleep in the room which he and his wife provided for me, but the books on the shelf by the bed were "accusing" me. Most of the books had been written by missionaries, people who had already translated the Word or who had been to the mission field and had written about their experiences. I began to compare my life to the lives that might be described in those books. I tried to make a mental list of what I had accomplished so far in life. I couldn't think of one important thing I had done.

Failure, failure, failure. I haven't done anything, I thought. *I'm thirty years old. I haven't done anything. I've never been on the mission field, and I don't really want to go there alone. I have never written a book. I have no husband, no children, no house, no car, and no career. All my brothers and sisters have those things. What is wrong with me?* These are the thoughts that filled my mind.

All my college and Bible training was reduced to one tactic in that moment. Someone had said that if you get in a very hard place, just tie a knot and hold on. I closed my eyes, hugged my pillow firmly, and concentrated intensely on the fact that God must be there, knowing that my focus on the Lord was all that was holding me together. It was a very long night with virtually no sleep. I pictured myself holding on to a big knot at the bottom of a long rope that was suspended out in space. The name of the space was "uncertainty."

The next morning, I told Harry and his wife how the books on the shelf had tormented me, and how I needed to get away to a completely neutral place, a place with no academics or missionaries of any kind. I knew I could not work, though I really didn't have any money. I couldn't go back to class, but I had no other goals, no frame of reference. Harry brought up the fact that I had been in the army and would qualify for help at the V.A. Hospital for free. I was thinking that maybe I could go there as an outpatient and get counseling.

A momentary glimpse of purpose ...

Before leaving the Wycliffe property to drive across town to the hospital, I had a conference session with several Wycliffe staff members. One was Ken Williams, the head of the counseling department. The bandage on his nose reminded me that teachers and students had prayed for him in chapel because he was battling cancer. I felt such compassion for him. I wanted to reach out, lay my land on him, and rebuke the cancer. I knew I would probably weep over him. *That probably wouldn't look very strong or spiritual*, I thought. I knew that I had been acting like a "basket case" and that people would probably consider my prayer to be invalid. Fear of man and unbelief swooped down like vultures to rob this momentary unction to pray for him.

I did not know it then, but that urge to pray for Ken was the real me, the Jesus in me trying to rise up and minister. It was the real call of God, the call to be used in seeing people healed. Think about it. Jesus healed people everywhere He went! Despite my Bible school training and five years of knowing the Lord, I was still trying to serve God with just my intellect. I would discover later that my world view had been making it impossible for me to function in my calling. The anointing of God was present for me to pray for Ken, but I did not yet grasp that the anointing of

God was my greatest gift. The idol of achievement had received my deepest worship and had left me useless. (It would actually be years before I would cherish the anointing and the authority to pray for the sick.)

Ken asked me, "What would you do if you could do anything?"

Looking back, I now realize that he was asking me about what career I would choose if I could pick freely. However, I took him literally and said, "I would crawl up inside a big hamburger and eat. I am so hungry. I want to eat, but I can't."

Thinking about it now, it probably really did sound as if I were crazy, talking about crawling inside a hamburger. The truth is, I was hungry and tired but could not eat or sleep. After this humbling interview, Harry drove me to the V.A. Hospital.

During the ride, I thought about the temptation that had come to me in the recent weeks to backslide. Silently, in the car, I made a mental pledge to the Lord. *If I have to go to a mental hospital to avoid going back into sin, I will. I'm not going downtown to find a man. I will walk in holiness no matter what the cost. No matter how bad it gets, I want to get to the root of what is wrong with me. I don't care what anyone thinks.* It comforted me to tell the Lord this because I could sense He was listening. I did not feel alone.

So, it has come to this?

I hoped that I would not be staying at the hospital. To actually *stay* in a mental ward would surely mean that there truly was something deeply wrong with me. On the other hand, I had no job or place to live. My siblings, all of whom were older, were married with families, houses, cars, and careers. I had none of those things, and here I was at thirty on my way to a mental ward for evaluation. Wow. It began to sink in that I might really be the bad apple in the lot, the defective model with a wiring problem.

After just a few minutes with the psychiatric doctor who interviewed me, she made a statement that was quite unnerving. She said she believed I was "on the verge of a full-blown psychosis." I didn't know exactly what a "psychosis" was, but it sounded very serious and frightening, like something from which you might not return. I hate to talk about this part, but I'm telling it because it might help someone. Her statement made me want to cooperate.

She asked about any unusual perceptions I might be having. I told her how street signs and trees often didn't look real; sometimes they looked like props that could be snapped off at ground level. I told her about the anxiety, the fasting, and the walks. I'm sure I listed my failures. This last conversation before being admitted to the hospital is now foggy, like a person's memory lapse right before a car crash.

She suggested that I rest in the next room. *Rest*! I was a bundle of nerves; it was light outside. They gave me a pill or two, and I was surprised that my nerves retired to let me sleep.

That was it. I woke up in a mental ward. Yep. All my thirty years of hard work had gotten me here. I had been wayward in college, but Jesus had cleansed me from all that. I thought that there must be something deeply wrong with me still, a flaw, some mental or emotional quirk that maybe could not be fixed. I thought maybe the wires in my brain were hooked up wrong, like a birth defect. My dad had frequently and jokingly said to my mom, "You're crazy." Well, I thought, maybe the so-called crazy gene had been passed to me.

Life in the mental ward

My street clothes were taken away, and I was issued beige and white, pinstriped pajamas. It was a constant conflict in my mind that I was a Spirit-filled Christian and yet in a mental ward. I had already walked five years very closely with the Lord, so I just kept reading my Bible every day and praying the best I could. My brother's wife gave me a lap desk, and I spent time reading the Bible, writing poems, drawing, writing letters, and keeping a journal. Eventually I was transferred to a different ward and given my regular clothes. I guess I was off the critical list.

I looked forward to bingo on Friday nights in the hospital basement with other vets. We could win tickets with which to buy snacks in the hospital shop. Eventually I went out with a couple hospital buddies on weekend passes to downtown Dallas. We would go to the top of the Reunion Tower to see the city lights, staying out of mischief. After just a couple hours of roaming in the city, I was usually ready for the hospital ward again. My nerves felt fragile, as if I would overload if there was too much going on. I was desperate for meaning and direction. I didn't want to be near anyone who was succeeding, unless it was just to be in church.

My sister-in-law also gave me a copy of Gail Sheehy's book, *Passages*, in which she decodes various rites of passage that we observe in America, whether we realize it or not. She explains how there are predictable crises in adult life. Many people think they have to accomplish certain goals by age thirty, by age forty, etc. A light began to flicker in my understanding that my goals had been shaped more by the culture than by the Word of God. Having lived overseas as a teenager, I knew how to step back from American culture and view it objectively. I began to see that my goals were primarily rooted in achievement, not in serving. I realized also that I was pressuring myself on a timetable that was not necessarily God's. I had thought that I had to have a husband, kids, house, car, and career by age thirty.

The secular versus the spiritual

Recently, to help me reconstruct the past for this book, I ordered all my medical records from that hospital. I was amazed to find that the hospital nursing staff had made daily records of my moods, activities, grooming, and even my comments. They recorded that I looked down on the group therapy sessions, thinking I knew more than any of those people. The group therapy sessions were very uncomfortable for me because the staff was educated in modern psychology, but they discussed nothing about spiritual warfare. Of course, they weren't paid to discuss the Holy Spirit's methods.

I associated only with my two hospital friends, a girl just younger than me named Denise, and a friendly guy named Gary who had a pickup truck. We were the three musketeers, usually talking about the Lord, strengthening ourselves in God. I did know a lot of Bible; and I was not getting much out of the counseling groups, which were totally secular in their approach. The group sessions made me realize that I was going to have to slug it out with the devil. There was not going to be a shortcut. Don't get me wrong about one thing, though. The kindness of the hospital staff came like a balm.

May I never be totally removed from the most humiliating day of my life. The memory of it will forever help me to care for people who are in limbo, in distress, in hopelessness. On a sunny, winter's day, about twenty of us "mental patients" went outside to play volleyball on the hospital grounds. There we were, perfectly healthy physically, but parading in our pajamas to the volleyball court next to the hospital. Anyone driving along Lancaster Boulevard that day could guess we were from the mental ward. I was hoping no acquaintance would recognize me. Time seemed frozen. My thoughts circled again and again. *Why am I here? What is wrong with me?* I was so disappointed in life, so tempted to write myself off.

I think now about a Bible verse in Romans 4 where Abraham believed God despite his circumstances. The phrase "in hope against hope" comes to mind. That day on the volleyball court, I held on to the knowledge that God is good. I just put one foot ahead of the other because I knew it would be a poor Christian witness not to try. I had tried so hard to serve God during the previous five years and could not see how it was fair that I was in those pajamas in broad daylight. I just let go and did what I had to do, trusting that God would not leave me there permanently. In the natural, I did not see how I would ever get direction or momentum in life again.

"Seek ye first the kingdom of God"

Fortunately, the above phrase (Matthew 6:33 KJV) had already been well etched into my mind. I requested rides to my church in Duncanville each Sunday morning and every Wednesday evening while living in the hospital. I knew that fellowshipping with other believers was going to be a key to finding God's will. It was very humbling because I was fairly sure even the teenagers at my church knew I was staying at the hospital. Despite this shame I felt, I was determined to seek God *His* way. I kept attending church, reading my Bible, praying, and talking about God to other patients. I prayed frequently in tongues to help push away confusion. The hardest mental challenge was that I had no future plans.

For exercise, I would walk by myself around the entire perimeter of the hospital, praying, singing, or meditating in Scripture the whole time. I figured that at age thirty, I was perhaps in the wilderness the way Jesus had been at age thirty, and that I was in a battle with some personal adversary. I just made all the right choices I could. I knew that my mother's mother had perhaps committed suicide by intentional drowning, so I figured that this might have something to do with my trouble. I wasn't going to cave in to something like that. I knew the Lord, and I knew the enemy's ways. I resolved that evil spirits weren't going to push me that far. Life wasn't making sense right then, but deep down I hoped it would again make sense.

My brother and his wife, both Christians, would come and take me out of the hospital for short visits to their home. My sister-in-law said it was good that I was getting help, that some people never do. They went out of their way to act as if my being in the hospital was a normal circumstance. I'll never forget their kindness.

When I had been in the hospital almost three months, Harry Bascom, the counselor from Wycliffe, came to visit me. He said, "I had hoped you would be out by now. You have good days and bad days. Why not just walk out on a good day?"

Gradually, I accepted his challenge. A random GI Bill tuition check came to me from Uncle Sam for several hundred dollars. Harry found a pastor's house for me to stay in. I began to think about asking my former boss for a job, working with young children in a very nice child-care center in Duncanville, not far from the pastor's home. I made plans to leave the hospital, even though it made me nervous to think about it. I knew I could not stay there, and nothing was really changing in my present state. I had heard that if you get moving in some direction, God will direct your steps.

Just before leaving the hospital I went cold turkey off the three medications that I had been taking while there — doxepin, lithium, and thiothixene (navane). The drugs had helped me to relax some, but they had also caused me to sleep through church. Also, I often felt as if my mouth and whole body were stuffed with cotton. I could not picture myself getting on with the will of God in that condition, so I stopped taking the drugs. Let me underscore here that I had a strong foundation in the Word and had already experienced the power of God on occasion. Had I not had this spiritual history, I don't think I would have had the faith to go off the meds. Also, looking back, I think I should have let my pastor know. At the time, I saw myself slugging it out with the devil in the wilderness.

Finally sensing God's direction

Backing up, I want to tell you what a still, small voice had been saying to me when I had been struggling at the Wycliffe Bible translation campus. When I had been so weak and tired at school, I would pray for direction. I had had this little, quiet idea always in the back of my mind. *Why don't you go live in Duncanville and work at the Enrichment Learning Center?* I would argue with that idea in my head. I'd argue that it was too humbling to work for minimum wage in a daycare center when I had a college degree. How would I afford a place to live on such a salary? I had no car. How would I get to work? It was too humbling, too complicated. I kept dismissing it from my mind. I thought that no one with a college degree, not to mention all the travel experiences I had had with my family, should work at a daycare center at age thirty. I kept wondering what my siblings would think if they heard I was working in a daycare center, not to mention my parents. All I could think about was what other people would think. Partly due to my upbringing, I felt uncomfortable unless I could impress people.

However, after three months in a mental ward, that job at that daycare center didn't sound quite so bad. I would have to work with preschoolers. Truthfully, I had always really loved small children. I had never even considered working with children as a career, though, because I thought I had to do something much, much harder in life than that. (I can't blame my parents, because my dad had tried ten years earlier to convince me to get a teaching certificate.) I had thought that even school teaching, especially elementary school teaching, was for "ordinary" people. I had wanted to do something "much more important, more intellectual, and loftier."

This pride, rooted in insecurity, which had shaped my goals, sounds ludicrous now. I remember thinking after college that people such as librarians, secretaries, plumbers, electricians, nurses, farmers—almost anyone without an advanced degree—were nobodies, "common workers." I had always thought I would get some kind of advanced degree and be an important *somebody*. It was a warped way of thinking that had come to permeate my world view. Later I would come to realize that all careers require learning, wisdom, and common sense. People have all sorts of gifts, not the least of which is the ability to serve others. Why hadn't I grasped this? The Bible says to get wisdom. I had never thought about wisdom. I had focused on getting recognition.

After three months in a mental ward, I decided that teaching in a daycare would be better than being confined to a hospital. I resolved that even if I had to scrub toilets, I wasn't going to let the devil trick me into staying in that hospital. I would allow myself to work in this daycare to avoid having to be in a mental ward. I had turned over the stone of trying to be a big shot; now I would allow myself to be just a regular person with goals that suited me. I didn't realize it fully then, but I was in the middle of learning this crucial lesson in the Christian life:

> There is a world of difference between our choosing
> what we will do "for God" with our intellect
> and choosing what He will do "through us" as we yield
> our entire being.

I went for the interview and got the daycare job back on the spot. I had to repent to my boss for having left that job about a year and a half earlier due to a trapped feeling. My boss, Kaye Aldridge, said warmly, "You have a mountain of potential on the inside, but it's as though you don't let it out."

Potential?—maybe, but I was only starting to have *humility*. It sounds like a paradox, but I had great insecurity and yet a haughty ego at the same time. I wanted to have very lofty plans, but I would not stick with anything that required repetition or that was sometimes mundane or boring. In fact, I had at that time a long history of leaving jobs, leaving majors, and leaving cities. I have since learned that all careers and callings include many, many moments of tedium. Gradually, I learned that with spiritual tools, one can make tedious moments rich in God. Prayer is one way. Meditation in the Word is another way. Getting this was huge for me. I learned that many small, seemingly insignificant moments can add up to rich moments.

To make a long story short, I took the job. It was part-time, so I took a church secretary job at the same time. I obeyed a Bible principle and sought godly counsel from a pastor/teacher friend, Allen Beck. I had to pick some direction, so without any feeling or warm fuzzies or strong desire, I set my sights to get a Texas teaching certificate to go with the degree I had gotten ten years earlier in Iowa. I had always liked children and had enjoyed helping them. For the first time in my life, I made a major decision based on common sense rather than on feelings. I would try to become a teacher. I didn't know what age or subject I would teach, but I would invest my efforts in children. Allen Beck, my pastor friend, suggested that later, if I still wanted to be a missionary, I could go to the mission field as a teacher of missionaries' children. This sounded balanced. Now I had a sense of purpose.

Let me pause here to say something obvious. All this trekking around the mountain could have been avoided if I had learned to listen to the voice of God and to obey it. He had tried to direct me to the daycare center months earlier, but I wasn't ready to obey until I had hit a new low. Now He had my attention. I was willing to follow His leading, His peace, no matter what.

New goals, intense resistance

I already told you that just before leaving the hospital, I went cold turkey off those three meds—doxepin, lithium, and thiothixene (navane). This approach may not be right for everyone. I did have quite a bit of Bible training and head knowledge about spiritual warfare. The combination of going cold turkey off the drugs *and* facing my new career goals was quite an intense chunk to bite off. There was tremendous resistance.

For example, two times at my daycare job I experienced complete stoppage of thought, where my mind drew a complete blank. It was as though my thinking was paralyzed and could not move in any direction. You might think this is restful. Well, it's not. It's quite terrifying. Fortunately, I had heard about this phenomenon during a Bible course at Christ for the Nations. I knew it was a symptom of a passive mind. My years of drifting, of doing what was easy for me, had produced passivity in my will and mind. To get hold of my thoughts, I had to call on the name of Jesus. Praise God that I knew this Bible verse: "The name of the LORD is a strong tower; the righteous runneth into it, and is safe" (Proverbs 18:10 KJV). I had to put total trust in this verse of Scripture. I pictured myself inside a little stone tower. I called on the name of Jesus over and over, and my thoughts came back to me. The warfare was very intense.

During this time I went for counseling with a Spirit-filled therapist. Everything we talked about seemed to point back to some teenage experiences. It had to do with a season in India, boarding school, and separation from my parents. I knew also that my temperament was prone to take things too seriously, so I had to confront that too. The main point I want to make is that when I opened myself up to the work of the Holy Spirit, He did gradually give me understanding as to when the roots of stress entered my life. This understanding was a key to my recovery.

I did go back to school to get a Texas teaching certificate. Eventually, I got a job in the daycare program of a Christian school. Later, I was hired as a classroom teacher in that same school. The first two years after the hospital were extremely difficult. To be totally honest, for many months it was like climbing a sheer cliff with no pickaxe. Day after day I would climb straight up an endless cliff, holding on to the bare rock, which was the Word of God. Life was one challenge after another. I was going back to do the challenges that I had run from in my twenties. I was re-patterning my choices, and there was no shortcut. My one solid mainstay was the Word, keeping my mind fixed on key Bible truths.

I had gone through my twenties as a single person, and I now went through my thirties single. I was regaining lost ground. I cried myself to sleep sometimes, but I now had a great teaching job in a Christian school and felt blessed at work. I was regularly in church and sang in the choir. I kept turning my sense of loneliness over to the Lord. I wrote songs. I sang for weddings and funerals.

I sensed that I was following the direction of the Holy Spirit, not some idea I dreamed up in my head. How was I able to connect with Him now? I had dealt with some roots, wrong mindsets, and wrong motives! I later married at age thirty-nine, had two wonderful sons in my forties, and became the pianist in a Spirit-filled church, which is what I do now. As a former teacher, I am involved with jail ministry and with music. God has brought all the threads together as only He can. As Psalm 139:14 says, "I will praise you because I am fearfully and wonderfully made."

What is a nervous breakdown, anyway?

I am happy to report that the counseling community has changed the term for "nervous breakdown." I'm glad because that expression in itself has always made me feel somewhat nervous. The new term is "disintegration." Some call the working-through process "reconstruction." I prefer these terms. Here's why.

You might think that a person who suffers from a nervous breakdown has some integral flaw, some wiring problem that can't be fixed. If a car breaks down, we know there is a mechanical problem. However, when a person breaks down, it can simply be due to wrong thinking. Wrong thinking can produce misdirected goals, obsessions, or disappointments that aren't taken in balance. One's mind-set can be so engrained that he doesn't even realize he *has* a mindset. Over time, a wrong mindset can leave you quite bankrupt, especially when your plans repeatedly don't pan out. A person may begin to have trouble even functioning. In truth, this warning is a blessing in disguise, if heeded.

Disintegration is what happens to a person when the goals, values, objectives, or perceptions that have sustained him in the past no longer work. A person can be laboring under the expectations of parents, of society, or of one's own false priorities. A person who has a breakdown is not laboring under what God is asking. Probably he or she cannot discern what God is asking. Jesus says in Matthew 11:30 that his "yoke is easy" and his "burden is light." We talk about people having blind spots. Well, sometimes I think our ears can be plugged, too. Our inner ears can be filled with wrong thinking, unable to hear or accept the simple instructions the Holy Spirit is whispering.

What to do if you think you are having a nervous breakdown

If you think you might be having a nervous breakdown, the very first thing I would do is counsel with a pastor or mentor who has a reputation for moving in the gifts of the Holy Spirit. The power of God can set you free from demonic oppression. This option may not be available to you if you are in an institution such as a prison or rehab facility. You might be able to write to someone you trust and ask for a visit or for prayer. I did not follow this advice I'm giving you now. I thought my pastor at the time would ridicule me, so I did not even consult him about the stress I had when studying linguistics. My pastor seemed almost irritated with me for struggling with depression. I really should have pushed past this feeling, which was probably just rejection operating in me.

There can be unique scenarios in which a person has just lost a child, or a limb. I think that intense distress would be normal in those situations. I'm not talking about this type of scenario. I'm talking about the slow-cooking mindsets that overtake a person, having brewed for perhaps years. One can labor so hard under false mindsets that it begins to drain all one's energy, joy, and hope. When things don't ever seem to pan out, over a period of years, great emotional fatigue can set in. Things can begin to appear unreal. There are medications which can help relieve the depression or anxiety. In some cases, shock treatment, or ECT (electro-convulsive therapy), is administered. This is a more aggressive therapy which is used in cases where medications may not be advisable, or where it is deemed that the patient may be in danger if a more slow-working approach is used.

If you are terribly anxious and need to buy time to work through your issues, you could take advantage of a doctor's help and recommended drugs. However, just know that no drug is a cure. You must realize that you really can straighten your thinking out and get out from under the false pressure with which the enemy is squeezing you. If you persist in the Word and claim your deliverance, it could be just a matter of time before your faith rises and you stand up and take dominion over fears and wrong thinking. The more foundation you have in the Word, the easier this will be. See the medications as a temporary form of relief so you can work on your root issues. I believe God wants to show people the very source of their stress. It usually involves a wrong mindset, a time of confusion in childhood. If you are a person who never does go off prescription drugs, there is no condemnation. God's love is big and can embrace any person who takes medication.

However, the reason that I am writing this book is to tell you that there is great power in God.

Also, I would never tell anyone to just go cold turkey off medications if a doctor's prescribed therapies are helping you. However, I am saying that you can so saturate yourself in the truth of the Word of God that your understanding of your own condition may become clear. You can enter a place in the understanding of God's power— the power in the blood, the power in the name of Jesus, and the power in the Word—that you can "be transformed by the renewing of your mind." (Romans 12:2). You can adopt a new mindset, a new set of objectives. When you do, it will be the real you. If life is one big chore, you can be pretty sure your agenda doesn't match God's; or your mindset doesn't match His. The Word of God is alive and can work changes in you (see Hebrews 4:12). Being on medications doesn't stop God's Word from changing you.

There is a French expression—*raison d'être*—or "reason for being." I believe that everyone who is undergoing therapy for depression should steadily immerse himself/herself in the Word and believe God to move him or her to a place of complete healing. You may find that the Holy Spirit will reveal to you that your perceived "reason for being" is off center. You may be serving idols, worshiping your children, trying to please other people more than God, trying to be perfect. It can creep up on you very subtly.

This book has resources that are based on a Biblical understanding of the power of God. Your thinking can be transformed, and thus you will be transformed, no longer laboring under some set of expectations that were never meant for you. During talks with women in the jail who are suffering from very extreme anxiety, some have admitted to laboring under agendas such as the following: always trying to make everyone else happy, always trying to live up to others' standards, always trying to be the perfect parent, or constantly obsessing over failures. Reading the Word can cause you to actually discover your own wrong agenda.

Getting at the root of the stress I felt

You may think my reason for having a nervous breakdown was shallow. Maybe you feel your pressures have been a lot worse than mine were. Maybe you grew up in a really messed-up home with addictions or perversions. We will get to testimonies like that in this book. I think that my issues revolved around my sensitive makeup and a longing to please my father. I actually never became aware of stress until my late twenties, probably because I ran from stressful situations. Then stress came like a freight train, swiftly from behind, leaving me paralyzed on the tracks of life.

In hindsight, one event in my teen years turned out to be fairly pivotal for me in terms of perceived security. When my brother and I were in junior high, our father accepted a position working in India and neighboring countries. His agricultural work helped boost food production in these struggling nations. As I entered high school, my mother, my brother and I traveled to India to join our father. During our time in India, my brother and I were usually in boarding school, away from our parents. Our parents made countless sacrifices so that we could have this unusual experience. For me, however, the lengthy separation from my parents, especially from my father, created a sense of isolation. Also, during this time, I was put on fairly heavy doses of female hormones to retard my growth. All teenagers have to survive adolescence, and it seemed we had to climb mountains, including the Himalayas.

The enemy seeks to derail children by confusing their thinking early on. When we went to India, with books all around, I felt a constant pressure to stretch myself to catch up academically to the standards of the boarding school. In addition, the missionary kids around me had grown up together and shared a closeness into which I could not really enter. This school was at that time primarily for children whose parents were from the West. We did have some Indian students, but most of my peers were from America, England, Scotland, Germany, New Zealand, etc. Several of our high school teachers had PhD's. They were amazing people, and their standards were high. The pressures of school, homesickness, and my own introspection were taking me toward an unhealthy mindset. I think I began to draw the subconscious conclusion that academics must be more important than relationships, that school was more important even than family.

As a young child, I had enjoyed a big house, a big family, and lots of animals on our two and a half acres in Iowa. I now felt surrounded by books and bookish expectations. Our school was located in the foothills of the Himalayas, which meant steep walks. My knees, which had already been dislocated numerous times, hurt when walking these hills. We had mandatory study halls for two hours each weekday evening in a large hall at the girls' dorm. When I did join my parents down on the plains for the cool winter months, there were no other young people with whom to interact; but there was homework. I was in India for only two and a half years, but it truly felt like ten years.

Looking back, I am deeply grateful for all these adventures in a foreign culture; but at the time I was constantly longing to be back home in Iowa. I returned to the U.S. with my mother to complete my senior year in my home town, but our father stayed in India another year. The last time I lived full time with my father was early in the eighth grade.

Later, in college, I kept looking for the closeness I had enjoyed with my father as a younger child. I looked to men for this. Once I became a Christian, I sought to win my father's affection with academic achievements. God has helped me to work through these layers, these patterns, so I could develop a secure closeness with God as my Father. I have found that with God the pressures are never over my head.

The great underlying irony of all this is that my father loved us deeply. Had he ever realized that I was pressuring myself to please him, he would have been saddened. Our parents chose to make the trip to India so as to give my brother and me the best possible exposure in life. We have an adversary, though, and he comes to distort reality. Despite the extreme devotion of my parents, I was laboring under some kind of emotional isolation.

God is always working out His purposes, even when we don't know him personally. One behavior emerged during the time in India which was to prove valuable later on. Because of homesickness and boredom, I spent long hours in my school's music building, just making up music on the piano. This was a place of peace and relaxation. Due to the emphasis our family placed on reading music, this undisciplined pastime seemed like a second-rate hobby to me. I was not good at reading music. Still, it was fun and engaging.

I had no way to know then that the skill of playing the piano by ear would someday help me assist during worship and prayer lines, when the Holy Spirit would be touching people's deepest needs. A hidden truth was this:

the wholesome outlet I chose in the music building was the real me. I did not have a personal walk with Christ then and was not drawing on the comfort of knowing that God was actually with me. However, He was leading me to play the piano by ear. This skill has become one of the most useful and enjoyable skills I have ever developed. It also opened the door to songwriting.

> Often the godly choices we make just to cope become the building blocks of our true calling.

Carol's Journal

As an example of how to process your own generational issues, I'm going to list mine. Four people in this book will do this. It brings great freedom to have an understanding of the roots that have plagued a person. You can cooperate with the Holy Spirit in getting them neutralized. Once you identify roots, let them go. Let it be permanent.

Generational curses (negative, repeating patterns)
- anger
- exalting education above walking in God's power
- hyperactivity (along with creativity, which is a positive aspect)
- knee problems
- depression, mental illness, patterns of regret
- early death—a great grandmother, a grandmother, a cousin, two brothers
- possible suicide in the case of one grandmother
- disease patterns such as heart disease, arthritis, glaucoma

Behaviors
- very hard spankings administered in anger by an adult
- cupping the hand over the mouth and nose of a crying child
- occasional outward displays of parental anger that could have been injurious (shoving, throwing things)
- tension in the home between parents, frequent arguing
- great emphasis on education, accomplishments, and travel
- emphasis on religion, not on God's power
  ➢ little emphasis on soul winning
  ➢ no training on how to move in the gifts or walk in authority

Mindsets
- Potential must be realized. Potential is huge.
- Talents must be developed. The highest possible level of education should be reached.
- Words—"You can be anything you put your mind to." (I don't remember discussions about "finding God's will for your life.")
- A *good* mindset that I want to keep: having seen so much suffering in India, I want my life to help make the world a better place.

Medical factors
- I went on hormones from age fifteen to age seventeen to stop growing.
- I experienced blood sugar swings in high school and in college.
- I had knee problems growing up, dislocating knees frequently.

Personality issues

- I was an auditory thinker in a large class that had to be quiet. I had to be drawing pictures, joking, or talking. Today I would be labeled ADHD. I was frequently reprimanded for causing a disturbance.
- I got along very well with music teachers.
- I must admit that I was generally sarcastic and rebellious.
- By nature, I am fairly introspective.

A trigger in life that set me on a downhill trend

Going to the boarding school in India as a teenager was a turning point. From this point on, life seemed hard and lonely. When I went to college, I dove off into the deep end, morally speaking. I was definitely looking for affirmation and a father substitute. I became a Christian at the age of twenty-five, after college. Though I cleaned up my lifestyle by God's grace, I still labored for several years to gain affirmation through achievements.

Choices I made after the hospital that turned things around

1. I decided to think on Scripture only once my head hit the pillow at night. I stuck with this until it became natural, like breathing. I quit planning my tomorrows on the pillow.
2. I sought counsel from spiritual leaders who knew me personally. When making a major decision, I would bounce it off a mentor. This does not mean that they made decisions for me. It just means that I followed the advice in this Bible verse: "Surely you need guidance to wage war, and victory is won through many advisors" (Proverbs 24:6).

3. I would not quit anything I started. I would not quit a job or a class until it was completed. I made good on my commitments, even verbal ones. Only with much prayer would I change a plan or a course. I attended church no matter what.
4. I accepted the fact that every assignment in life has some boring, tedious aspects. When a trapped feeling would come upon me, I would deal with it, often calling on the name of Jesus, speaking the Word, or speaking in tongues.

My gifts

- I enjoy studying languages.
- Playing the piano, singing, and writing songs are enjoyable pastimes.
- Being part of the worship team at church is a musical and spiritual adventure.
- Talking and praying with women at the county jail is like having lots of sisters. I can share the lessons I've learned.
- Writing letters to people in prison brings satisfaction.

Goals

- My husband and I are committed to helping our college-age sons get the best possible start in life.
- I want to leave a positive legacy of having influenced others toward heaven. I plan to continue publishing songs.
- By staying hooked up with a strong church, I believe that we as a family will be able to help impact many people, perhaps even people overseas. We can do this by giving in whatever way is needed: financially,

through prayer, through encouraging, through moving in the gifts—it's all about sharing Jesus.

You may be dealing with issues that seem much more challenging than mine. I included my story to describe what it feels like to have a nervous breakdown, or disintegration, and to recover. I have included other people's stories in this book to amplify the truth that you can overcome any habit or past hurt. I do hope that you can identify any bitter roots and that you can let Jesus assist you in removing them. Paul put it this way in Hebrews 12:15: "See to it that no one falls short of the grace of God and that no bitter root grows up to cause trouble and defile many." This is made possible by cooperating with the healing work of the Holy Spirit.

Summing up: Let the Root of Jesse
supplant every other root.

(Jesus is referred to as the "Root of Jesse" in Isaiah 11
and in Romans 15)

A Matter of Life or Meth

Laura

Rock Bottom

I had been using meth so long that it no longer helped me feel better. I had hit rock bottom, then hit it again, several times. However, I kept doing meth. I had lost everything but my two daughters. I had lost my best friend, my house, my land, my money, and my reputation.

I knew that if I did not stop meth, I would die or kill myself; and I just could not do that to my girls. They had already been through so much. One daughter had slit her wrist, and the other had tried to overdose on drugs. It was as if the three of us were walking through land mines. We all had pieces missing.

I had gotten to the point that meth wasn't giving me the euphoria which it had at first. I felt horrible whether I used or not. If I would come down off the meth, then I would have to face the pain of abuse, which was overwhelming. Most recently, it had been marital abuse. What got gotten me to this point?

Love vacuum

My childhood was a time of isolation. I remember being molested by my mother's brother at ages three, four, and five. That is the only touching I remember. Even my mother never touched me. There was no love or affection, spoken or unspoken, in our home. The silence would be interrupted by words from my mother such as: "You are ugly. I wish you had never been born. You will never be anything." My kind and generous father influenced me positively; but he worked out of state most of the time, so I felt abandoned. My mother seemed cold; they were opposites. There was no balance in the home.

When my parents became Christians, they were very zealous. There was no interaction in the home, no games, no playing cards. I wasn't allowed to see any friends. My mother was very religious, and the only social contact I had was with people at church. I remember that my mother seemed to be filled with anger, even rage. This was not seen in public.

Because my father succeeded in business, we didn't lack for anything. It was never openly said, but I grew up assuming that money gives power. I assumed also that I should get higher education, especially since my mother said I would never be anything. Unconsciously, I became obsessed with proving that she was wrong. I would seek higher education and have money. I would be somebody.

Because of our family's orientation toward church, I decided to attend Bible college after high school and to become a missionary. I even married our minister's son. He admitted to cheating on me; so a year after marrying him, I divorced and left Bible school and the church. By the age of twenty-four, I had married and divorced two more times. Secretly, I was into drugs, alcohol, and promiscuity. On the surface, I had a good job and great friends who knew nothing about my dark side of hurt and pain. After the first marriage, I went completely wild for seven years.

The model mother

In my late thirties, I met my fourth husband, with whom I later had two children. Alcohol played a major role in our family life. I had left all other bad habits behind, but I thought the alcohol was normal. To the community, I was a model mother, very involved with my daughters' activities. My influential husband and I appeared to be pillars in the community. I immersed myself in my daughters, my husband, and our business ventures. This mirage did not last. My husband's serious drinking problem was the catalyst for physical and extreme mental and emotional abuse. After fifteen years of marriage, I had to divorce him. Ironically, my husband was speaking the very same words over me that my mother had.

One year after the divorce, still on the search for security and love, I found a new boyfriend who then introduced me to meth. I experienced euphoria. It helped me forget pain, and it was fun. This boyfriend proved to be quite psychotic, so I left him to protect myself. I got into an association with a relative of his, thinking this person could protect me. He then became my new best friend. He was a meth cook, but I did not realize he was also a very heavy user. At first, he never did meth in front of me.

At this period in my life, I began to withdraw from society. I owned many acres of land in the country, and my new boyfriend and I started to cook meth together. I then had a pure product any time I wanted, and as much as I wanted. Most meth users don't have access to such an unlimited supply. I had money from my divorce, and my reinvested stocks brought in a lot more.

We used aliases and would share our meth with our closest friends. In return, they would go out and buy the supplies we needed for cooking. Meth gave me a sense of being powerful, even invincible. Whatever a person's strengths are, meth enhances that. However, it also enhances weaknesses, making you even more vulnerable in your weak areas.

For example, I had always been an honest person. To me, if people hid things, they were liars. My opinion was that if you're ashamed to do something, you shouldn't do it. The meth made me even more open and transparent than usual, so I wasn't as careful with our secret information as I should have been.

Soon my place was under surveillance twenty-four hours a day. We could not leave the property without being followed. We were afraid to let our guard down, afraid even to sleep. We would stay on meth and be awake for two or three weeks straight, nonstop.

I began to feel rage against my ex-husband. Meth intensifies hate. The rage and pain grew. I couldn't do enough meth to stop the pain. I didn't trust anyone now. I couldn't stop the drugs, and I wanted to die. I did more drugs, an unbelievable amount. The habit became huge, consuming me.

Death Valley days

Six years after the divorce, I was out of money. I had been arrested several times with heavy fines, bail money, lawyer fees, and jail time. Meth was no longer fun nor was it killing the pain. Eventually, I lost everything—my money, property, possessions, and my best friend.

The police had found some meth, and I had taken the fall for my boyfriend in the hope that he would not go to prison. He went to prison anyway, and I was put on probation. I loved him. This felt like the end of the end. I had no place to go. My girls were in my life, but they did not know what was going on with me.

I did have another friend who was a meth dealer and cook. I went to his place, so depressed. I couldn't die, I couldn't even overdose. This friend supplied me for two years. When my boyfriend got out of prison, we got together and were doing meth again within three months, on some other people's property. My girls still did not know what was going on. My boyfriend treated my girls with a fatherly kindness, and they loved him dearly.

Still, it was clear that I could not stay in this relation-ship with my boyfriend and keep doing meth. We would go to prison or die. If I were to leave my girls by death or by prison, I felt certain they would not survive it. They had had so many struggles by this time, including suicidal behavior. Despite all my problems and secrets, the girls depended on me for strength, love, and acceptance.

During this time, I kept hitting rock bottom, surviving somehow. Even though I had not been convicted, I could not get a job or housing due to drug issues. I moved in with one daughter, praying constantly.

Encounter on the road

One day, I was driving my daughter's pickup when the hood flew up. At the side of the road, a man who was in AA helped me, and he talked about the AA program. I had tried everything but AA, so I gave it a shot. The decid-ing factor was my children, whose ages were fifteen and twenty-one. I chose life. I chose my children. I chose God. I could not destroy my children. I walked away from meth and toward life. I threw my meth paraphernalia into a dumpster and flushed the drugs down a toilet. I began attending AA meetings three times a day.

I did that for one year. Much of the time I had to walk to the meetings. Like a pit bull, I held on. I read Christian books, such as *Wild at Heart* and *Ransomed Heart* by John Eldredge. I read *The Shack* by William Young. I found a Living Bible, which I could understand, and journaled. Other than my girls, there were no people in my life. I kept calling various agencies to get help, but there was always some obstacle, some reason why I could not hook up with a program. This went on for three years. It was as though God cornered me with Himself for these three years—alone.

I began to discover that God is love, unlike the impression of God that I had had as a child. I had always thought that God was angry with me, disappointed with me. I discovered that I was worthy, that God could forgive me. He had even known me before I was ever born. He knew my heart, that I had never wanted to hurt anyone but myself.

Jesus said, "I am the door" (John 10:9 KJV).

During this period of drawing close to God, I did have one relapse of three months. Then I closed the door on meth completely. I persisted in calling agencies, trying to get help. One day, the doors opened. God answered my prayers by letting me meet the most amazing people. I believe that I had become grounded in God and that God knew I would not totally look to people anymore to rescue me or to give me an identity. For two years I received Christian counseling at no charge. A Christian agency provided rehabilitation to help me get back into the work world. How my life has changed! I have been free from meth for six years.

Now free from drugs and other addictive behaviors, I am involved in work I really enjoy. God has promoted me to an administrative position in an agency that helps people. I have found a church where I can grow and establish relationships. God is restoring me as a mother and grandmother. I have forgiven myself and others.

Laura's Journal

Generational curses
- anger, rage
- rejection
- depression
- sexual abuse, lust, impurity
- idolatry, religious spirit
- codependency

Behaviors and influences in the family
- anger, rage
- abusive language
- fear in the child
- rejection, loathing of a child
- emotional abandonment, lack of emotional protection, absence of a parent
- sexual abuse to a child by a close relative: lust, impurity
- low self-esteem: resulting behavior—striving to please through accomplishments, education
- dysfunctional family, not together, not communicating
- religious spirit: emphasis on outward appearances
- idolatry—oaths taken in Masons and Secret Sisters by my grandmother

Mindsets and words
You are not worth anything. You have to prove your worth.
You have to be very religious and educated. It's all or nothing.
Love must be earned.

Medical factors
   Physically, I was very healthy growing up.

Personality issues
   I always was very honest. I felt I had to tell the truth about everything.

A trigger in life that set me on a downhill trend
   I cannot remember a time when I felt love or hope as a child.

Steps to freedom
1. I chose to live. It would be the best possible life. I want to make a difference. If I am going to live, I am going to have a purpose.
2. God had to be in my life. I had had everything. None of it satisfied. I had a hunger for God.
3. I "cleaned house." I would leave negative influences. I would be alone if necessary.
4. Focus. I will be in God's Word. This is so important to me.
5. When I am helping somebody else, then I am the strongest.

Gifts
•   I have always been able to identify with everyone, regardless of age or station in life. People say that I am a strong and loving woman. They say I am non-judgmental.

Goals
•   I want to make a difference for hurting people.
•   I am believing for total restoration in my home with my children.

My new mindset
- I am a warrior. I relate to Scripture verses that talk about standing strong, winning against the adversary.
- I live today, minute by minute. I am never alone.
- It doesn't matter how I feel. What matters is God's Word. It never changes.
- God knows I've always had a heart. I've always wanted to help people.
- Life is not a race. Your journey is your own. Everyone gets "there" at his own rate.
- There is no condemnation. There is hope. God cares. There are people who care.
- The spiritual world is more real than this world. You have to want it from the heart, more than anything.

Some favorite verses

"So if the Son sets you free, you will be free indeed." John 8:36

"Never will I leave you; never will I forsake you." Hebrews 13:5b

"Greater is he that is in you, than he that is in the world." 1 John 4:4 (KJV)

"Yea, though I walk through the valley of the shadow of death, I will fear no evil: for thou are with me; thy rod and thy staff they comfort me." Psalm 23:4 (KJV)

"For God hath not given us the spirit of fear; but of power, and of love, and of a sound mind." 2 Timothy 1:7 (KJV)

"As far as the east if from the west, so far hath he removed our transgressions from us." Psalm 103:12 (KJV)

"For with God all things are possible." Mark 10:27b (KJV)

"And ye shall seek me, and find me, when ye shall search for me with all your heart." Jeremiah 29:13 (KJV)

"Fear not: for I have redeemed thee, I have called thee by name: thou art mine." Isaiah 43:1 (KJV)

"You are precious to me, and honored, and I love you." Is 43:4b (The Living Bible)

"Yes, says the Lord, I will be found by you, and I will end your slavery and restore your fortunes." Jeremiah 29:14 (The Living Bible)

Child Abuse, Alcoholism, and Codependency: Sebastian and Monique

Monique

At thirty years of age I weighed three hundred pounds, my husband was an alcoholic, and my third marriage was failing. My husband's drinking had gotten so out of control, and the confusion in our home had become so great that we had separated. My girls (from a previous marriage) were begging me to take them to church. Other people were giving the girls rides to church. About the last thing I wanted to do was go to church, but I promised my girls that I would take them to church if I could get an eight-to-five job. Well, I got the job and didn't want to disappoint my girls. We began attending together.

Unlike previous churches I had attended, this church was a place where I was getting fed spiritually. I was under heavy conviction. I began to sense that God wanted to restore my third marriage. I was actually hearing God. One day there was a sermon about Peter's getting out of the boat to walk to Jesus on the water. Everyone has always criticized Peter for being impulsive and fearful—for sinking. What stood out to me was that even though Peter began to sink when he took his eyes off Jesus, Jesus still took his hand and lifted him up. Even though Peter's faith wavered, Jesus still helped him not to sink. This truth really hit me. I felt God was saying that He would help me if I tried to restore my marriage to my husband Sebastian. God would be with me, and it wouldn't depend on me alone

I felt that I should confront Sebastian about his drinking. *Confront?* I had never confronted anyone in my life. I had always tried to please, to keep everyone else happy. For years I had been stuffing all my emotions down and

138

had made food my substitute for whatever was missing. I had never really done anything for me.

The secret I had stuffed

How did I get this way? There were no problems in the home that I knew of or remember until I was two or three, when my parents divorced. I didn't know my dad. Then my mother got pregnant out of wedlock, so she married a second time out of a sense of obligation. That marriage lasted seven years.

When I was about nine or ten, my mother married for the third time. This man molested me from about the age of nine or ten until I was thirteen. I knew he didn't want my mother to know. I was afraid of him. I would stay at a friend's house whenever I could. I stuffed all my hurt feelings inside, acting happy and bubbly. I began dieting at the age of ten because my stepdad would tell me, "You look like your fat aunt." I felt as if I needed permission to breathe.

Finally, when I was sixteen years old, I told my mom about the abuse. She sat up in bed and said, "I knew it. If you would have told me when it happened, I would have left; but now I can't." That was it. My stepdad had become a Christian, so she figured there was nothing she could do. So, at sixteen, I just had to deal with it—no counseling, no asking forgiveness, no help, no closure.

That same night that I spilled the truth to my mom, I actually tried to confront my stepdad. He defended himself, saying that his older brother had molested him, and that this was why he was that way. I knew it was not an adequate excuse, that it didn't make things right. There was nothing I could do, though. I got no support, carrying all this inside.

Aiming to please

Something that had helped me keep my world together was music. I had played the clarinet from fifth grade to the beginning of high school. Then I was put into private school, and my mother put me into modeling school. Not having music at this new school left a big void. I was not allowed to date outside my race, but I did date on the sly. I thought about going to our pastor for help, but he seemed kind of wishy-washy. Besides, since our family attended church, I knew it would be a huge embarrassment if I told about my abuse issue. I didn't feel I could disgrace our family in front of all the church people. I didn't want to disappoint people.

In my senior year of high school, I got engaged to the boyfriend my parents approved of at the time. I realize now that I was manifesting codependent behavior, always putting other people's wishes first. I would give myself away, martyr myself. I would assume responsibility for others' feelings and behavior. I thought, "If you're okay, then I'm okay." I would minimize, alter, and deny how I felt.

This relationship ended. Then I got with an old boyfriend that I had secretly dated in high school. We married, and I found out two weeks later that I was pregnant. My husband was unfaithful, so I had a second baby because I felt I needed someone to love who would love me back. I was taking all kinds of abuse from this husband. At times he would drag me by my hair. He was very good at doing physical abuse in a way that left no visible marks.

More turbulence

Then I got pregnant with my third baby, my third daughter. When she was six months old, I began nursing school. When I was away from the house, my husband would talk negatively about me to the girls. Because of all the abuse, I knew I had to get them out of the situation. Once, when we were separated, he took all three girls; I had trouble getting them back. The ages of our little girls were four years, two years, and eleven months. My husband insisted that he should get custody of the girls. Finally, he agreed to let me keep the younger two, but he would take the oldest child. The physical abuse toward me had gotten to a point that I knew if I did not leave him, I was going to end up dead. That's when I made the agonizing choice to let my oldest child go on his terms. This way I would stay alive and still be here for them all.

At the end of my first semester of nursing school, I left him. I stayed in school, but I chose to go after men and dump them. I would remain detached from them, staying in control. I also felt detached from close family. I got into relationship addiction, hiding my pain. I was afraid to trust anyone. I would bring the men home when my daughters were at my mother's. I would date guys to fix them. I was overweight, so I didn't blame guys for treating me badly.

That's when I met Sebastian. He did drink, but he was nice. I was able to share all my stuff with him, and he could open up to me. We clung to each other. We moved in together and got a house. In 2000 we were married. Sebastian then opened a bar of his own, since he had been a bartender. This caused total chaos in our house. That's when my weight went over three hundred pounds. Sebastian's bar closed, but he went to work in a friend's bar.

His drinking was now way out of control. We separated, and I moved in with a friend who was also a single mother. This was my lowest point—depressed, overweight, and having another failed marriage. When my grandpa died, Sebastian did come to see us. I moved into Grandpa's house with my girls. The girls and I would go to church, and I was getting back with God. I didn't know it, but Sebastian was occasionally visiting the girls because he loved them.

Sebastian's Story: Time in a Bottle

I came from a good, Christian family, a long line of people who know how to serve. In my family tree you'll see military people, nurses, charity workers, and hairstylists. People in my background have been people of strong faith, forgiveness, and faithfulness, creating a great spiritual heritage. I think Proverbs 22:6 (KJV) sums up my family. "Train up a child in the way he should go, and when he is old, he will not depart from it."

Regarding pressure, I never really had any pressures in the home. My parents supported every decision I made.

Everyone has always supported me through the good and the bad. I have never passed blame on my family for my behaviors or consequences. The open door may simply have been that there was alcohol in my home. My dad drank responsibly, and several uncles drank frequently. There was always a beer or two in the fridge. My sampling started at age fourteen.

One incident with my dad may have added to the deception about alcohol. He had served in the military; then he began working out of town as a truck driver when I was fifteen. He was absent a lot. He was fairly strict, which I am actually thankful for now. Usually he didn't let his hair down very much. Once in my late teens, my dad and I drank a few beers and had a heart-to-heart talk, the first one we had ever had. Maybe in the back of my mind I drew the conclusion that beer is okay because it helps people open up.

Beer drinking reached a new height by age seventeen. Getting people to buy it for me was easy, especially since my girlfriend was older. By age eighteen, I was headed toward "out of control." I married right out of high school in a rush to become my own man, yet not a man at all. By the time I was twenty, I had for sure fallen victim to addiction. I was staying up until all hours of the night, with or without friends, drinking and having what I thought was a good time. Sometimes I was passed out in the back of my truck, so my wife would come out at 2:00 or 3:00 a.m. to see if I was still alive.

Even the birth of my first son did not slow me down. At age twenty-one, I would go through two or three cases of beer during the week, buying an extra case just for Saturday.

At age twenty-two, I began an alcohol-induced affair that would lead to a divorce. This affair resulted in a second marriage and the birth of my second son. I was so full of guilt and shame for leaving one child behind that I tried to be a better father for my second son. Three years into this marriage, which had been founded upon addiction, things went wrong. This time it was my wife who had the affairs. Fighting, drinking, and drugging were always going on. I sometimes used marijuana, occasionally cocaine.

Since I was carrying much guilt about my failures, frustration and anger set in to the point that I was dangerous to myself and to others. I would rip doors off hinges and break things. After five years, this marriage also ended in divorce. My second wife's addiction had progressed to the point that I got custody of our son, my second son. The patterns continued so that by age thirty I married for the third time.

Now my socially-oriented personality began to mesh more than ever with the bar scene. I was working lights and sound for a local rock/blues band and living that lifestyle. Having been a bartender/bouncer for a number of years, I had always wanted to be everybody's friend. My new wife Monique and I would throw big parties and pay for all the beer and food. All this experience gave me the bright idea to open my own club in 2000. This job created so much chaos at home that by January of 2002 I had lost the business and my wife of less than two years. We separated.

July 7, 2002 — My day of decision

During the separation, I would secretly visit the girls. I knew Monique was going to church. After seven months of separation, on Sunday, July 7, 2002, my wife Monique came to my house to tell me she was willing to give our marriage another shot. People need support when kicking addiction, and she was a support to me. That day she told me that she would get back together if I would make two promises. I had to stop drinking, and I had to go to church. She was surprised when I agreed to do both. I felt her support; it was the boost I needed. We had an open time of sharing about our past failures and hurts. We connected. That Sunday was a very blessed day for me, having my wife there with our two daughters from her previous marriage. We picked up the pieces and brought all our kids under one roof again. I had been out drinking the night before, but this day marked my new beginning.

Reconciled

Monique

From this point forward, we have had no more separations. I have been standing on 2 Corinthians 9:13, a command to forgive. I have forgiven my stepdad, my ex-husband, and my mother. I keep on forgiving. I pray for my mother that the cycle of dysfunction will be broken.

I elected to get stomach bypass surgery to help me lose weight because I was on nine medications at once. After the surgery, I was able to stop all nine medications. Sebastian did not require me to get the surgery, but he supported me. I knew he would love me whether or not I would choose the surgery.

Monique's Journal

Generational curses
- anger
- pride/rebellion
- depression, mental illness

- inability of a mother to show love to a daughter (goes back to great-grandmother)
- rejection, inferiority
- dysfunctional relationships in the family
- obesity
- dyslexia

Behaviors, conditions and influences
- anger, rage
- cursing, profanity
- physical and emotional abuse
  - ➤ verbal abuse
  - ➤ slapping, punching, hard or uncontrolled spankings
- sexual abuse by a step-parent, pornography, perversion
- overeating, food addiction, obesity
- smoking despite asthma
- yelling, throwing things; inability to deal with normal frustrations
- strife, arguing, bearing grudges, silent treatment
- separation, divorce
- low self-esteem
- passivity, fear of making mistakes
- poor spending habits, welfare, worrying about money
- pride, prejudice, racism
- importance and self-worth defined by physical appearance (parental pressure to participate in modeling and beauty competition)
- obsession with high achievement, must prove worth through education
- unreal expectations for children
- anxiety, irritable bowel syndrome
- confusion, mental illness, emotional imbalance
- depression, regret

- suicidal tendencies
- dyslexia
- learning difficulties (in mother and sibling)

Mindsets and words
- perceiving any statement as a direct challenge
- overly sensitive to the motive or attitude behind others' words
- reacting with an attitude: "Do you think I'm stupid?"

Medical factors
- obesity
- high blood pressure, heart disease
- asthma
- gastro-intestinal reflux
- irritable bowel syndrome

Personality issues
- highly controlling personality even at a young age

Trigger

When I got married to my first husband, I entered into such physical and emotional abuse that I became totally beaten down, with no hope. I gave up thinking things would ever be different.

Four choices I have made since reconciling with Sebastian

1. In order for us to reconcile, it meant letting go of some of our other relationships, friends that did not like the "new us." That was hard since some of these people were like family. In Celebrate Recovery, we say, "Change your playground and your playmates."
2. I also have to make sure to keep God as my focus. I can't look for my salvation in my husband. He is our spiritual leader,

and I have to make sure I do nothing to take that role away from him. This takes much prayer and is a daily process!

Stepping out on faith is a very scary thing. It is something that makes you fully rely on God, not self. However, letting God have control of my present and future is the best thing that could ever have happened to me. When I try to take this role back, it ends in failure. Letting God be in control provides me with an amazing freedom. I don't have to worry, because God's got this! Matthew 6:34 says: "Therefore do not worry about tomorrow, for tomorrow will worry about itself. Each day has enough trouble of its own."

3. The one thing I do every morning is recite the "Prayer for Serenity" in its entirety. I recommend doing this to get started. Also, when you do it, mean it.

God, grant me the serenity
to accept the things I cannot change,
the courage to change the things I can,
and the wisdom to know the difference.
Living one day at a time,
enjoying one moment at a time;
accepting hardship as the pathway to peace;
taking, as Jesus did,
this sinful world as it is,
not as I would have it;
trusting that You will make all things right
if I surrender to Your will;
so that I may be reasonably happy in this life
and supremely happy with You forever in the next.
Amen.

—Reinhold Niebuhr

Gifts
- serving, compassion
- nursing
- forgiving spirit
- ability to "never meet a stranger"
- I am able to listen to anyone; I can talk to people
- Communication skills come in very handy with Celebrate Recovery and nursing.
- singing; love for music

Goals

I'd like to be a life coach and reach out to more women in recovery, sharing Jesus Christ. I hope to have a ministry to women who have suffered from rape or physical abuse, perhaps volunteering in a shelter.

Sebastian's Journal

Generational Aspect

My parents used their time wisely and were good influences overall. I'm saying that my home was a positive climate. At present, though, I do have several cousins who may be borderline alcoholics. Any curses that came into my life were pretty much my own choosing. My heavy drinking was my own choice, like veering off.

A little pride may run in my family. We can talk openly about certain things, but we keep some personal issues under the surface. Mostly, we are a fun-loving family that can laugh and have great fun when we are together. Signs of deeper problems have not always been noticeable. When we are together, we feel love, joy, and peace. If someone did feel compelled to share something personal and difficult, we would probably cry together and pray together, making us stronger as a family.

Behaviors and curses which I brought upon myself
- anger
- rage
- fear
- depression
- lying, illegal practices
- low self-esteem
- failure
- obesity
- lust, impurity, perversions
- substance abuse, addictions
- codependency
- adultery
- desertion, abandonment
- worshiping achievement, education, status, works (This was my own hang-up.)

The ungodly mindsets I had to overcome
- I have to do some great thing to prove my worth as a person.
- Every family has a black sheep, and I'm it.

Medical factors
- obesity
- diabetes, mid-thirties
- strokes (2) at age thirty-eight (with full recovery)

Personality issues
- I like to be around people.
- When I was younger, I always wanted to be a people-pleaser.
- Socializing centered on alcohol.

Trigger
- There was always alcohol in the home.
- The fact that my dad wasn't around much in my later teen years might have been a factor.

Words from Sebastian about getting free and staying free

As I stepped into sobriety, the church was a major factor. I have always utilized the church as my main source of influence. I sought guidance and counsel through our pastor at the time. My wife had been praying for me a lot, as had my godly mother. God's grace and power were coming at me from all sides.

I didn't belong to a support group right away, but eventually I did attend AA meetings to gain a better understanding of the twelve steps and their history. I used to say, "I am an alcoholic." Now I am leader/coordinator with Celebrate Recovery (CR). CR has twelve steps, too. We say, "I have *struggled* with alcohol," or name whatever the battle has been. That way, we describe the sin; but it does not define who I am. I am free.

My marriage is now God-focused, and the five teenagers we have between us get along. I know it took long, hard prayer on the part of my wife and my mother for me to turn around. As my relationship with God was restored, His plan began to unfold. I had felt like a black sheep; but as the redeemed of the Lord, I went back to school in 2006. Today I work as a substance abuse counselor. For four years I have been a leader/coordinator, alongside my wife, for a Celebrate Recovery group, a twelve-step program. We also work with Christian Men's Job Corps and Christian Women's Job Corps, helping people get rehabilitated in life, using spiritual principles from the Word. I am thankful, and I know I have been positioned to prosper.

Five choices I have made to get free and stay free: (by Sebastian)

1. I kept remembering that God and my parents wanted something better for me.
2. I realize that formerly I wanted to drink or drug at any cost. So now, no cost is too great for me to remain sober. I will remain sober at all costs.
3. I stay in God's Word and attend church because I know that focus is necessary for effective faith.
4. I picture myself as the husband and father God intended me to be.
5. Through Celebrate Recovery, I work a faith-based, twelve-step recovery program and facilitate a CR meeting for others.

Gifts
- service
- compassion
- patience
- discernment
- leadership
- prophecy
- writing, communication

Goals
- I hope to do Celebrate Recovery as a fulltime ministry.

Sebastian's Word of Advice

If you go through recovery, you may go back home to your family and get the cold shoulder — you know, when people don't think you have changed. Relapse can occur before you actually fail. You have to catch it in your mind — that first hint of negative thinking. If you can, get yourself to a support group (being around people who can relate); it can be a great source of strength. Celebrate Recovery is one such support group. The best aspect concerning CR is that it is based on Scripture.

Please be sure to enter in your thoughts in the final pages of your Journal section. You can keep this journal and use the format for later tune-ups. This book is my journal, in a way. I will be using it to help steer people into hope. I believe it can be a handbook you can use to help others pinpoint and shed generational baggage and get on with the process of world-changing. If you would like to contact me to let me know what part of this book helped you the most, I would highly value that feedback. Just contact me at <u>longlink@sbcglobal.net</u>.

May God's richest blessings be on your life, Carol Joy

Helps

Part 1

Receiving Jesus Christ as Savior and Lord

If you are about to ask Jesus Christ into your heart, this will be (hands down) the most important decision you will ever make. Here are verses from the Holy Bible that instruct us about salvation.

Revelation 3:20—Ask him in.

"Here I am! I stand at the door and knock. If anyone hears my voice and opens the door, I will come in and eat with him, and he with me."

Jesus is literally knocking today at the door of your heart. All you have to do is to invite him in. He will come in and fellowship with you.

Hebrews 13:5—He will stay.

"Never will I leave you; never will I forsake you."

Once you ask Christ into your heart, He will never leave you. He will indwell you forever.

1 John 1:9—He forgives us.

"If we confess our sins, he is faithful and just to forgive us our sins and will purify us from all unrighteousness."

Your conscience is probably telling you that you have done wrong things. The Bible calls wrong thoughts and actions *sins*. Just agree with God right now that you have sinned, since Romans 3:23 (KJV) says this: "For all have sinned, and come short of the glory of God."

Once you have confessed your sins, they are forgiven. God's peace can flood a soul that is right with Him. The devil will try to drag up sins in your thoughts, but resist such thoughts. Stand upon the Word in believing that you are forgiven. Assurance will grow. Don't accept condemnation. Jesus paid for your forgiveness.

2 Corinthians 5:17 (KJV)—You are a new creation.

"Therefore if any man be in Christ, he is a new creature: old things are passed away; behold, all things are become new."

Hebrews 9:22—Blood had to be shed.

"Without the shedding of blood there is no forgiveness."

You just need to understand that it is the blood of Jesus that makes you right before God. You will never measure up one hundred percent to God's standards unless you receive your righteousness by faith. That's what you will do every day of your life.

1 John 5:11-13—We have assurance of eternal life.

"And this is the testimony: God has given us eternal life, and this life is in his Son. He who has the Son has life; he who does not have the Son of God does not have life. I write these things to you who believe in the name of the Son of God so that you may know that you have eternal life."

From now on, you will not stand on feelings. You will stand upon the Truth in God's Word. You *do* have eternal life, and you *are* going to heaven.

Matthew 7:21-23 — Make Jesus Lord of everything.

"Not everyone who says to me, 'Lord, Lord,' will enter the kingdom of heaven, but only he who does the will of my Father who is in heaven. Many will say to me on that day, 'Lord, Lord, did we not prophesy in your name, and in your name drive out demons and in your name perform many miracles?' Then I will tell them plainly, 'I never knew you. Away from me, you evildoers!'"

In order to walk in the blessing of salvation, it is vitally important to make Jesus Lord. It is not enough to just do lip service to Jesus. He expects one to follow Him, to obey the Word and to obey one's conscience. It is not based on legalism, but on a relationship. God's will is that we walk in obedience.

How to Grow in Faith as a Christian

- Read the Bible. Study it. Memorize verses that help you. Meditate in it. Walk in it.
- Pray without ceasing.
- Be in church and serve.
- Witness for Christ.
- Always be filled with the Holy Spirit, walking in holiness.
- If you do sin, confess it, brush yourself off, and move on in total forgiveness.
- If you are having a struggle, or need to make a big decision, seek godly counsel.

As your faith grows, you will know how God thinks. You will find that you can do the works of Jesus, having been given His authority. You will see others set free. The greatest deeds you will ever do in life will be deeds that influence other people to draw closer to God. The greatest words you will ever speak will be the very words of God.

Part 2

The Baptism of the Holy Spirit
(With Evidence of Speaking in Tongues)

N o discussion of spiritual warfare would be complete
without the presentation of the gifts of the Spirit,
including the gift of tongues. The Holy Spirit has a personality, a way of working. The gifts of the Spirit are also
called the "operations" or "workings" of the Spirit. They
are not meant for personal glory; rather, they are meant
to build up the body of believers. Some relevant passages
to read are Acts 1 and 2, Acts 19:1-7, 1 Corinthians 12:7-
11, and 1 Corinthians 14. Paul hoped that everyone would
speak in tongues as he did and expressed this.

Receiving your heavenly prayer language is an important step in learning to serve God and in not leaning on
your own understanding. Your tongue is the rudder that
guides the ship of your life, a metaphor used in the book of
James. Praying in tongues is a way in which to surrender
the tongue, even the mind, to the work of the Spirit. The
apostle Paul prayed in tongues regularly, and in the book
of Acts you can see he frequently laid hands on people
so they could receive the baptism of the Holy Spirit with
tongues as evidence.

The baptism of the Holy Spirit is referred to at the start
of all four Gospels, possibly because the writers wanted the

believer to understand the difference between the baptism of *repentance* and the baptism in the Holy Ghost, or in *fire*. John's baptism was the baptism of repentance, turning from sin. Jesus is the one who baptizes people in the Holy Ghost and fire. Jesus had breathed on the disciples (see John 20:22) and had told them to receive the Holy Ghost. Then, after His ascension, it was recorded in Acts chapter 2 that the Holy Spirit was poured out and they spoke in tongues.

One of the key evidences of Jesus's baptism is speaking in tongues. I believe that every Christian receives the Holy Spirit at salvation; but not all Christians know how to yield their vessels, allowing the Holy Spirit to operate through them as described in 1 Corinthians 12. Even as a Christian, we can resist the work, or operations, of the Holy Spirit and try to serve God our way, in our own strength. One may be bound by the fear of sounding foolish. This resistance is rooted in pride and in fear of man. It helps a lot to be in a church where the leaders understand and move in the gifts of the Spirit. I like to think that my church is a sacred workshop of the Holy Spirit, where we are all learning more and more how to yield and be used by the Spirit.

Jesus told His followers to tarry (wait) in Jerusalem, that they would receive the "promise." He was referring to the promise spoken of in the book of Joel, that God would pour out His Spirit in the last days—that sons and daughters would prophesy, that old men would dream dreams, and that young men would see visions. I believe that the baptism in the Holy Spirit is related to this outpouring in the last days. The baptism in the Holy Spirit, with speaking in tongues, opens you up to a level of yieldedness that invites a new dimension into your life. If you have not yet operated in your prayer language, you can begin on your own. You can ask God to baptize you in the Holy Spirit, and then pray in tongues by faith. If you are saved, you already have the Holy Spirit. It may simply be time to let Him out of a box. At first, you might say just one syllable. Some people experience a surge of tongues. One can also sing in tongues.

You'll get your tongue loosened with practice. Praying in the Spirit will build up your spirit man. You never have to worry about tongues' being from the devil. Paul would never have encouraged anything that was of the devil after his conversion. See the words of Jesus (found below) as He encouraged people to ask God for the Holy Spirit. I think He knew ahead of time that religious people might later have a fear of certain gifts, especially since the Jews had walked in so much legalism. They got upset just because Jesus healed on the Sabbath!

If you have been a Christian for years but have never really experienced the power of God or seen His miracles flowing from your life, I believe you will want to open your heart and mind to the following Scripture: "Which of you fathers, if your son asks for a fish, will give him a snake instead? Or if he asks for an egg, will give him a scorpion? If you then, though you are evil, know how to give good gifts to your children, how much more will your Father in heaven give the Holy Spirit to those who ask him!" (Luke 11:11-13 KJV). Of course, at this time, Jesus had not yet ascended to the Father, and the Holy Spirit had not yet been poured out as after His ascension. Tongues were poured out on people after Jesus left this earth in bodily form.

I believe that Jesus was assuring us in the passage above that the Holy Spirit's operations are not some evil manifestations to be feared. If God gives us the Holy Spirit, He will also help us learn to flow with the Holy Spirit in a way that will bless others. As long as your desire is to please God, your heart will not be led astray. Why would the devil want you to pray in tongues? When we pray in the Spirit, we are really praying according to God's will, not inventing our own agenda. We do it by faith. Yes, the devil has his counterfeits; but when you are calling on God in Jesus's name to steer you right, the enemy will have no access to your prayers.

When I first began to pray in tongues regularly, I would tell the enemy to leave, in Jesus's name. I would praise God in English, then speak in tongues, then praise God in English again. I wanted to make sure that nothing I was doing was of the devil. With time, I had such a handle on what Paul taught about tongues that it was no longer a battle.

One great advantage of praying "in the Spirit" (praying in tongues) is that the Holy Spirit can guide your thinking. I cannot tell you how vital my prayer language was when I came out of clinical depression and began to set realistic goals for myself. I would sometimes wake from a very confusing dream, or I would be perplexed about a decision to make. I would pray in my prayer language out loud; and after a few minutes I could feel the Holy Spirit taking hold and giving me direction in my thoughts. One can also pray very quietly or silently in tongues.

Most of the workings of the Holy Spirit involve the tongue. We read in James that the tongue is like a little rudder that drives the ship. It also can be a little fire that destroys the forest. I believe that using the tongue to speak in tongues is a way of surrendering this important little member to God. I have noticed that people who yield to the Holy Spirit and pray in tongues are often more likely to move into a realm where they also learn to pray with spiritual authority. This can pave the way for miracles.

Should everyone speak in tongues?

Some people claim that Paul said that not everyone needs to speak in tongues. This is a misconception. There is a difference between praying in tongues privately and delivering a message in tongues in a public meeting. As you read through the book of Acts, you will find that people spoke in tongues when hands were laid on them in faith, and they yielded to the baptism in the Holy Spirit. On the other hand, in 1 Corinthians 14, Paul is describing a completely different setting, that of a public meeting. Here he instructs that only two or three should speak out in tongues, then wait for interpretations. (If people who are developed in the gifts are present in a worship service, a word may be delivered first in tongues, then in one's natural language.)

Referring to this public setting in 1 Corinthians 14, Paul asks with a touch of sarcasm, "Do all speak in tongues?" If you study the context, you can easily see that he is underscoring the need for moderation in public meetings to maintain order. It would be chaos if everyone spoke out in tongues in public meetings. There would be no time for the preaching of the Word. That is why he implied that not all should speak in tongues, but he meant only in public. In this chapter (1 Cor. 14:18) he expressed that he prayed often in tongues, more than most people. He was referring to his private praying. He clearly wanted everyone to speak in tongues, but perhaps not in public, necessarily.

If I had to choose between the nine *fruit* of the Spirit (Gal. 5) and the nine *gifts* of the Spirit (1 Cor. 12), I would probably choose the fruit, just to make sure I am like Jesus. However, we don't have to choose that way! We can have both the holy and loving character of Jesus *and* the gifts of the Holy Spirit. Why wouldn't we want everything God holds out? Do I just want to be nice in God, or do I also want to walk in power, doing the very works of Jesus? Good food for thought.

As for entering into the baptism of the Holy Spirit, this can be done through the laying on of hands or when no one else is present. Some people are baptized in the Holy Spirit when they are alone. I received my prayer language in a prayer line after being immersed in water. Ultimately, it is God who baptizes us in the Holy Spirit; and we receive by faith. All God's great gifts are received and exercised by faith. That goes for salvation, for healing, for deliverance, and for the baptism in the Holy Spirit. If you want to pray in tongues, begin with one syllable. God will give you another one. Speak that. We speak as God gives us utterance (Acts 2:4). As I said earlier, you can also sing in tongues. In some churches, people sing together in the Spirit; and this is truly heavenly.

Your Journal Pages

1. List generational curses, patterns, or strongholds which
   you suspect have run in your family line.

2. List accompanying behaviors, influences, or conditions in your family which you believe may have affected or shaped you adversely.

3. List mindsets or words which you need to discard. Or, you simply may want to record the new mindsets or confessions that you are adopting.

4. List any unique medical factors or personality issues which seem relevant to your development. Give these over to God, reminding yourself that God made you the way you are because it gave Him pleasure.

5. Try to identify a life trigger, a time or event that seemed to cause a downhill trend. Give it over to God, and let it go. Forgive any people you need to forgive, including yourself.

6. Take authority over the negative. Use the prayers that speak to you. Command, renounce, plead the blood, resist, pray the prayer of agreement, confess the Word, pray in tongues, praise, seek counsel or write letters, and stand. Having done all, stand. Mix your faith with the methods of praying you choose. Use the type of prayers that seem to click for you, which release your faith. Go ahead and record the prayers you have prayed. Keep standing.

7. List giftings that run in your family tree, and especially in you.

8. List several "steps toward change" that are working for you or which you want to implement. You may want to refer to the steps listed by Carol, Laura, Monique, or Sebastian.

9. Dream a little. List goals which you would like to accomplish. Setting both short-term and long-term goals makes them seem more attainable.

10. Close your eyes. Picture yourself as you want to be. Describe the person you want to be. That's you.

"Now to him who is able to do immeasurably more than all we ask or imagine, according to his power that is at work within us." Ephesians 3:20

References

Baker, John, *Celebrate Recovery*. (Grand Rapids, Michigan: Zondervan, 1998).

Bonhoeffer, Dietrich, *The Cost of Discipleship*. (Nashville, Tennessee: Broadman and Holman Publishers, 1998).

Carothers, Merlin, *Prison to Praise*. (Escondido, California: Merlin R. Carothers, 1970).

Goodwin, Doris Kearns, *Team of Rivals*. (New York: Simon & Schuster, 2005).

Nee, Watchman, *The Spiritual Man, Volume Three*. (New York: Christian Fellowship Publishers, Inc., 1968).

Sheehy, Gail, *Passages*. (New York: Ballantine Books, 1976).

Thompson, Dr. Carroll, *Possess the Land*. (Dallas, Texas: Carroll Thompson Ministries, 1978).

Waltz, Dr. Mitzi, *Adult Bipolar Disorder*. (Sebastopol, California: O'Reilly and Assoc., Inc., 2002).

About the author....

Despite the advantages of having traveled around the world as a teenager, and having attended secular college and Bible college, the author found herself emotionally bankrupt at age thirty. That is when the Bible became more than a devotional book. It became the only tangible rescue line to grasp over a chasm—the chasm of uncertainty. Now, years later, having become a teacher, a church musician, published songwriter, wife, and mother, she is mentoring women in jail and in prison. She has found that most people who cycle repeatedly into failure, or who just don't reach out for their dreams, are laboring under generational baggage. She brings this practical handbook to people who are tired of spinning their wheels.

The author lives in Texas with her husband and two college-age sons.